BARRIERS

THE LIFE AND LEGACY OF
TOM EVANS

D1450871

LOIS HOFFMAN

ISBN: 978-0-578-79430-3

A portion of the proceeds from book sales donated to the National Wildlife Federation.

HSP
PUBLISHING
HSPPUBLISHING.NET

TABLE OF CONTENTS

FOREWORD

I n my career, I have been privileged to work with, know and observe a number of accomplished individuals who have been great conservation leaders.

Prominent among them is Thomas B. Evans, Jr.

I have enjoyed Tom's company over the 12 years we've been acquainted. In the process, I've learned a great deal from him on how he effectively marshals people and arguments to achieve his goals of protecting the natural and the human environment.

Barriers describes many of his legislative and policy achievements, especially in the environmental arena. I am honored to write the foreword and share my perspectives on Tom Evans's skillful environmental advocacy.

I first met Tom early in 2008 through an introduction by Jane West, a mutual friend and accomplished environmental attorney who had recently worked successfully with Tom in the Briny Breezes land-use dispute in southern Palm Beach County, Fla. Jane said Tom had asked her to introduce us, as he wanted to discuss his wish to become more involved with the Florida Wildlife Federation (FWF).

We met briefly at an Everglades Coalition event, followed by a more involved meeting at his seasonal residence in Delray Beach, and we hit it off professionally and personally. Soon thereafter, Tom joined the FWF's volunteer Board, where he served well for a decade. He and his wife Mary Page provided valuable assistance to FWF in many areas, and they continue to be supportive of my current work with the North Carolina Wildlife Federation. Through Tom, I was introduced to many interesting and influential people who were able to support FWF's conservation work further.

An early example was in 2009, when Tom provided critical aid in getting support from the governor of Delaware and former colleagues in the U.S. House of Representatives for pioneering climate legislation. This legislation was strongly supported by the National Wildlife Federation, and it passed the House, but unfortunately failed to move in the U.S. Senate.

I've met with Tom at home in Wilmington, Del.; Tallahassee, Orlando and Delray Beach, Fla.; Washington, D.C.; Virginia Beach; and New York City, reaching out to allies and potential allies in efforts to promote coastal conservation policies. We also met with officials in the Interior Department and the U.S. Fish and Wildlife Service on the need to protect, modernize and expand the Coastal Barrier Resources System and further extend its concepts to floodplain policies across the country.

Tom clearly recognizes the need to build strong and diverse coalitions of organizations and people from all walks of life if we want to secure passage of environmental legislation. He befriended Democrats and Republicans alike, from Tip O'Neill to Ronald Reagan, and has always been able to bring people together on behalf of his causes.

These causes have included helping secure the passage of the Alaska Lands Act; reducing pressure to over-harvest timber in the Tsongas National Forest; keeping oil and gas drilling off the caribou calving grounds of the Arctic National Wildlife Refuge; and passing laws to stop ocean dumping of cruise-ship garbage. The pinnacle of his environmental achievement was the nearly unanimous Congressional support for the Coastal Barrier Resources Act. With help from President Reagan's, Tom secured the support of the interior secretary, and the bill was signed into law.

Tom has extraordinary people skills, taking a genuine interest and treating all he meets with respect. On the streets of St. Petersburg, Fla., he provided advice and encouragement to young advocates for solar energy expansion and opposition to oil and gas drilling expansion in the eastern Gulf of Mexico and the Arctic National Wildlife Refuge. And I once saw him help a very confused man on the street in Delray Beach find his way home.

I have noted the obvious affection and respect many members of Congress still feel for Tom. Watching Tom deliver Congressional testimony, I recognized that he naturally has what my mother always encouraged me to develop in myself: the "ability to walk with kings but not lose the common touch." People working in the Congressional dining facilities, in fine social clubs and on Amtrak to and from Wilmington; people at Tom's favorite local diners in Delaware, New York, D.C. or Palm Beach County – whoever they are, they always have warm and comfortable exchanges with him.

Watching Tom prepare for an important meeting of allies or opponents or making a case to policymakers is entertaining and instructive.

If it's an environmental issue, Tom typically meets with interested advocacy organizations, but he doesn't stop there. He looks for opportunities to engage people and groups across society. Those within communities near a controversial project site and municipal workers – including fire, police, emergency management, water and sewer, infrastructure, transportation and others – all have perspectives on how well existing infrastructure can sustain new, intensive development. He seeks out allies and pursues alternatives to poorly sited projects. He knows a lot of people and understanding their views and concerns is important in developing and communicating about achieving better environmental outcomes.

Over 12 years of working alongside Tom on environmental issues, I've observed that he's particularly skilled at sizing up issues and people and helping put together effective coalitions to achieve desired objectives. Tom knows how to get things done. He has the gift of gab, but he also knows how to listen – and that includes listening to the very insightful advisor he has in his wife, Mary Page.

Tom also has lots of friends who have provided key support to his causes. It's always fun to work with Tom in preparing for an event, whether it's reviewing his statement before a presentation to Garden Club of America members, working on film preparation and scripts for "Battle for the Barriers" with Teleduction's Sharon Baker and Pascal Dieckmann, preparing for Congressional committee testimony or meeting with prospective donors or other charities with mutual interests.

Tom has classic good manners; he is well educated and knows history, politics, business and human nature. He is an excellent writer and an exacting editor. He is invariably polite and kind but does not suffer fools gladly. As with almost all people with political experience and gravitas, he knows when to keep his own counsel, when it's best to be silent and when to push through the open door. I have never observed in Tom any expression of prejudice of any kind, and, despite having left his youth behind him and coming from a well-heeled background, he's empathetic to others and maintains a youthful enthusiasm.

These traits have aided him in his personal, political and professional life. His advocacy on behalf of the environment is constant and unwavering, and all the environmental work I have seen him perform has been done without compensation. And advocacy on behalf of the environment is time-consuming and requires true commitment.

Maintaining the integrity of the Coastal Barrier Resources Act (CBRA) for almost 30 years, in shifting political winds, has been a challenging endeavor for Tom, but largely a successful one. CBRA and related programs are early and successful examples of climate adaptation to rising seas and worsening storms and are classic examples of common-sense conservation. The legislation makes sense environmentally and economically, saving American taxpayers billions of dollars.

In addition to maintaining CBRA's integrity, Tom supports expanding the program to other areas, such as the Pacific coasts of the United States. Likewise, CBRA concepts can be expanded into the interior of the country by removing subsidies that support or promote development in areas known to be flood prone.

Tom has consistently supported funding for updating and digitizing CBRA mapping and utilizing the best technology to scientifically map flood zones to help make the best flood zone and coastal policy decisions. This, again, saves taxpayer dollars, reduces risk to people and property, and protects habitat.

Tom supports green infrastructure, protecting wetlands and natural areas to help buffer the built environment from disastrous storm damage. He was prophetic in recognizing early on that subsidies that promote intensifying development in areas in harm's way are a bad investment of taxpayer dollars. Tom has allies in the reinsurance industry, as well as free market and taxpayer organizations, all of which share a goal of reducing the massive risks to which many of our coastal and low-lying communities are exposed.

As he advocates, it makes sense to turn areas subject to repeat flood insurance claims into parks, wildlife refuges, greenways and beach or water access sites that can be sustainably enjoyed by the public as recreational areas. Greening shorelines, protecting habitat for fish and wildlife, buffering storm impacts by creating new open lands and moving development back from the shoreline to higher ground – all these endeavors make sense, especially with documented and projected sea-level rise and intensifying storms.

The reader of *Barriers* will gain insight into the remarkable career of Tom Evans and learn about a number of his achievements, which sometimes were hard won but won nonetheless. Tom's determination to make a critical difference for the natural environment is a fire that burns brightly within him and which will never be extinguished. His environmental legacy shines and illuminates a path for us all to follow.

~ Manley Fuller

Manley Fuller is Vice President of Conservation Policy at North Carolina Wildlife Federation and previously was president and CEO of Florida Wildlife Federation from 1997 to 2019.

PREFACE

On a quiet cul-de-sac in an upscale area of Greenville, Del., with neighbors the likes of Joe Biden, a storm door stands open despite the freezing temperatures. The man in the entryway, though having had his share of birthdays, exudes the joyful presence of a 6-year-old on the first day of summer vacation. However, Tom Evans, former United States representative from Delaware, is serious about his role as environmental protector and political connector.

Inside his home, art adorns the walls. Tom's wife Mary Page is a nationally recognized artist with works in several museums and prominent collections. Along with her artwork, he explains, hangs work of other artists, many famous, some fledgling, whom they feel called to support. Support and generosity are themes that reveal themselves again and again in the people and causes they support.

Past the kitchen, which smells of Mary Page's famous lemon cupcakes, sits Tom's office. The space is not much bigger than a corner booth in a diner, but every inch is filled with his life's work. One file cabinet neatly holds over 100 speeches given throughout his career — eulogies for friends and colleagues, talks at universities, speeches at prayer breakfasts and testimony in Congress. Another cabinet contains op-eds and press clippings he has written, or which have been written about him. Still another catalogs photos of the myriad of people – the famous and not-so-famous – he's connected with over his life. Even at 89, he's adding to his collection.

Tom is eager to share stories of his time in Congress — the people, the places, the awesome power of the experience. A stroll down the hall just outside his office is like a walk on the famed red carpet, except instead of famous actors to the left and right, politicians tell a tale from decades ago. A commendation from President Jimmy Carter, a handshake with Gerald Ford, a Jamie Wyeth sketch of John Mitchell and a framed letter from Ronald Reagan line the walls (along with a photo of legendary golfer, Arnold Palmer). That Tom is in many of the photos testifies to his time in the center of the political universe. Each photo carries its own memory, and he hasn't forgotten any of them.

Much of this book centers on Tom's political career. His time in Congress may have been relatively brief, but his presence in Washington spanned decades. And the environmental policies he helped implement altered the politics of his time. It chronicles his deep passion for the environment, but more than that, it illustrates his deftness for relating to people. Unlike the politics of today, he managed to bring people together — to find common ground. He built lasting relationships through relentless effort and his fierce determination to include everyone in the process and gain support for any cause he supported. If you wanted something done – money raised or people on your side – you called Tom. His work is a roadmap for those entering the political sphere and those determined to make Washington work for the people.

Tom's story doesn't start or end with his political life. What he was to become politically started earlier in his career and his life. Even as a young boy, his propensity for risk-taking developed into the courage to speak his mind to the most powerful people and entities in the world.

Much of what he did after leaving office defined him just as much, as his overflowing file cabinets attest. He hopes his story inspires the next generation of influencers and politicians and reshapes the discourse in Washington, as well as the political climate in the country. And, of course, he hopes to inspire the continued preservation of our fragile and natural lands for years to come.

PART I

EARLY YEARS

CHAPTER ONE

DELAWARE, VIRGINIA AND BACK AGAIN

Tom was born on November 5, 1931, in Nashville, Tenn., to Thomas, Sr. and Hannah Hundley Evans. They lived in Old Hickory, Tenn., and, at the age of seven, his family moved to the quiet downstate town of Seaford, Del., where his father was a works engineer at the new DuPont Company nylon plant and a member of the school board. His mother was active in her church and the town. Their prominence in the community served as both a model for Tom and a source of early connections that catapulted him into adulthood.

From an early age, Tom recalls, generosity was drilled into his head by his mother and drilled into his heart even before he started school. He listened to his mother read stories that focused on caring about others and watched her good works in action. He absorbed well his mother's words — remember that you're fortunate and have a responsibility to help others — and ever since he has made a commitment to be as generous as possible with his time and treasure.

Beginning at age seven, his mother and father took him to the golf course, where he gained skill and passion for the sport. It also prepared him to use this venue for connecting with friends and soon-to-be friends throughout his life. The long fairways and beautiful greens served him well in his youth, as they would in the years to follow, by allowing for uninterrupted time to listen and ask questions as well as gain perspective on issues important to each member of his foursome.

When Tom was young, he spent summers on the sandy beaches of Rehoboth Beach, Del., and lived the remainder of the year in the riverside town of Seaford. He was inextricably linked to the water. As a boy of 12 or so, growing up along the

Nanticoke River, he once climbed in a small boat with a peanut butter sandwich and just enough gas to get him into trouble. He motored out to the Delaware Bay within sight of a passing freighter which frantically waved him back toward home. The story speaks to his love of the water and tendency toward risk-taking, a trait ripe for taking action despite the possible consequences.

He attended Seaford High School in Delaware and later Woodberry Forest School in Virginia, where he excelled at sports — undefeated in wrestling and a top pole vaulter and golfer.

In addition to his athletic ability, others saw leadership qualities in him. One of his teachers at Woodberry Forest approached Tom and asked him to stay at Woodberry and serve as senior prefect.

Most of Tom's relatives had attended Episcopal High School, a boarding school in Alexandria, Va. Tom chose Woodberry Forest because it had a golf course, of course. He would later serve on the board of his beloved school.

After leaving Woodberry Forest, Tom chose the University of Virginia, where he studied political science as an undergraduate and continued on to law school. Tom's competitive nature followed him throughout college and defined him as much as his charm with people. While there, he continued pole vaulting until he made the Virginia golf team his second year and led his team as captain. Under his leadership, his team won the Eastern Intercollegiate Championship.

Athletics were a crucial part of Tom's life. Not only did he enjoy being outdoors, whether waterskiing, playing tennis, or skiing in Vermont and Colorado with his family, Tom was highly competitive. He often played mixed doubles during his time in Washington. A few times he was teamed up with Supreme Court Justice Sandra Day O'Connor. "She was a competitive player and very gracious on and off the court," Tom said.

In addition to sports, Tom was president of St. Elmo Hall, a fraternity at the University of Virginia, and served as an officer of the Student

Council and the Interfraternity Council. His energy and enthusiasm also stood out as he was selected as one of two out of 50 students vying for the UVA cheerleading squad, an all-male group at the time. He fondly recalls trips to the University of North Carolina which had the "best-looking cheerleaders" in its mostly female squad. Watching him reenact a cheer he led some 68 years ago, it stands to reason that Tom continues to cheer for people and causes, as his friends so often attest.

Golf, leadership and his association with UVA anchored him for the post-graduate phase of his life. Upon graduation, he clerked for Charles L. Terry Jr., former chief justice and eventual governor of Delaware, setting Tom up with an impressive resume to start his career.

In the late 50s, in the midst of the Cold War, a booming economy and increasing racial tension, Tom was president of the insurance and benefits firm Evans and Associates Inc. in Wilmington, Delaware. The firm's impressive client list included the Delaware Medical Society, the Academy of

Lifelong Learning, the Delaware Bar Association, the Delaware River and Bay Authority, the Wilmington Police, the Wilmington Fire Fighters and many more. He developed relationships with the top businessmen in the state and involved himself in church and service organizations, often rising to leadership roles, such as outreach committee chair for Christ Church in Greenville, Del. as well as chairman of the Every Member Canvass.

Building on the success he had in the business and non-profit world, it wasn't long before he took his energy and enthusiasm into the political arena.

CHAPTER TWO

ENTRANCE INTO POLITICS

Tom began his passion for politics working on Barry Goldwater's failed bid for president in 1964, who lost to incumbent Lyndon Johnson. He quickly increased his involvement in Delaware Republican politics through his fundraising efforts on various campaigns and his work on the Delaware Republican Finance Committee (DRFC). In 1970, Tom was elected Republican National Committeeman and served in that position until he was elected to Congress in 1976. The committeeman position held the keys to many of Tom's connections and whetted his appetite for an increasing role in politics.

In 1967, Tom was appointed as the head of the Nixon for Delaware campaign. His fundraising efforts were so successful that he was promoted by Richard Nixon to serve as chairman of fundraising for the Mid-Atlantic, Florida and Puerto Rico. He built a reputation as a prolific fundraiser and leader. He caught the eye of national leaders in the Republican Party. His list of connections grew, as did the opportunities for making a greater impact.

He pursued each position with ardent determination, often working 60-70 hours a week to get the job done between his business, busy political calendar and a growing family at home.

In 1969, the year following the riots over Martin Luther King Jr.'s assassination and subsequent National Guard occupation of Wilmington, Tom was tapped to head the Delaware State Development Department by Governor Russell W. Peterson. He focused on the economy and tourism and worked with educational institution Delaware Technical and Community College to ensure a ready workforce for attracting businesses to the state. He got to know even more prominent members of the Delaware community, including longtime friends John Rollins, Hal Haskell and Tyler McConnell.

During his tenure at the Development Department, Tom met the Rev. Leon Sullivan, Baptist pastor, social activist and founder of the Opportunities Industrialization Center (OIC). The OIC sought to empower African Americans by encouraging large corporations to hire them. While Gov. Peterson recognized the economic and social promise of the group's effort, he faced a major political hurdle in his desire to have Delaware be the first state to support the OIC with state funding.

At the time, Delaware politics was split between moderate, business-oriented Republicans in industrialized northern Delaware and rural conservative Democrats below the C & D Canal.

Peterson, from northern Delaware, needed a champion to persuade those from the decidedly more conservative southern part of the state. Tom was the perfect messenger. As a moderate conservative and former resident of Seaford to the south and current resident of the more populated northern part of the state, Tom was asked by the governor to take his plan before the Delaware General Assembly to advocate for economic opportunities through funding the OIC in Delaware. His efforts were successful. Tom built on his reputation as someone who could relate to people on both sides of the aisle and, in the case of Delaware, from both sides of the Chesapeake Canal.

These were a few of a series of successes that cemented Tom's status as a rising star in the Delaware and national GOP.

In 1971, Tom accepted a position on the Republican National Committee (RNC). Secured primarily through friendships with members on the Republican National Finance Committee, he also befriended long-time supporters in Republican circles. Bob Dole was awarded the national chair position, and Tom took on the operational challenge as RNC general chair of administration and organization. Mary Page quipped at the time, "I hope some of Tom rubs off on Bob Dole. I know Bob Dole won't rub off on Tom." Not everyone laughed.

During his time at the RNC, Tom oversaw the nomination and re-election efforts of Richard Nixon amid the president's growing Watergate scandal. The RNC ran coordinated-yet-separate efforts with the Committee for the Re-election of the President to re-elect Nixon. The RNC emphasized positive things about Nixon's international work, connected with political organizations, identified voters and led Target '72, a get-out-the-vote (GOTV) effort. Their goal focused on and succeeded at running a clean campaign to re-elect the President.

In a closed meeting with key Republican governors after the 1972 Nixon victory, Tom spoke privately about the campaign and how the Committee for the Re-election of the President (pejoratively called CREEP), led by John Mitchell, may have taken much of the credit for Nixon's re-election. Tom suggested that CREEP downplayed the clean and effective campaign efforts by the RNC in the victory. The story leaked to the White House and Tom was the only member of the RNC not invited to the Christmas party that year.

Tom engaged in conversation with President Nixon

As Tom's amicable nature often facilitated, he later became friends with Mitchell. Years later, after Mitchell served a prison sentence for his role in the Watergate coverup, Tom helped him to secure work with one of his clients. He also aided in organizing Mitchell's funeral when he died and gave one of the eulogies.

Prior to the funeral service in November 1988, Tom remembers hearing a booming voice saying, "Where's Evans?"

Tom walked across the room to Richard Nixon and said, "Sorry to have to be here under these circumstances."

Nixon responded with, "Who's here?" Tom ran down a list of those in attendance including the press secretary under Nixon, Ron Ziegler, Sen. John Warner and Jerris Leonard, an assistant attorney general in charge of civil rights, along with other Congressmen and notables.

"Where's George?" Nixon continued, referring to newly elected president George H.W. Bush.

"He's with Will Farish in Delray Beach," Tom said, while mentioning the toll the election took on Bush and the need for some time off.

The former president snapped back, "He should be here. Mitchell made him." Mitchell recommended that Nixon appoint Bush as the

Ambassador to the United Nations and later as the chairman of the RNC.

Tom answered, "You're right, sir. He should be here."

Tom's penchant for connecting with people set him apart regardless of issue or affiliation, as acknowledged by John Mitchell. Time and again, he rose to leadership positions, not only because of his passion and enthusiasm, but due to the persistence with which he operated. Whether working on a campaign with colleagues during his tenure as outreach committee chair of Christ Church, or on the board of Ford's Theater in Washington, Tom dedicated himself to each cause as if it were the only thing he had to do.

Tom demonstrated networking prowess within each organization and was adept at cross-pollinating the groups. His Rolodex overflowed with the powerful connections he used to make an impact. When someone asked a favor of him, he often said yes — whether it was delivering speeches or eulogies, chairing a committee or running an event. He was known as a man you could count on to get things done — especially fundraising. His easy way brought people to his side and money to his causes, political and charitable.

His tireless advocacy sometimes left him at odds with some around him. Yet Tom's ability to listen deeply and convincingly persuade brought lasting change on important issues and respect from those around him. In 1974, as Delaware chairman of the United Negro College Fund, Tom chose to hold its annual event at the exclusive, nearly 120-year-old Wilmington Country Club, where he served on the board. Although some at the time questioned the impact of inviting the approximately 150 African Americans along with 150 white people to the event, they admired Tom's courage to integrate the club after its long history of exclusion.

With an upbringing encouraging service for the public good and his connections with the most powerful in political circles, Tom was poised to step out of the background into the center of the political stage.

PART II

GENTLEMAN FROM
DELAWARE

CHAPTER THREE

ON THE HILL

In his first campaign brochure, Tom encapsulated his vision: "I'm running for Congress to help get Americans working together again." Once elected, he delivered on that promise — to Delaware and the country.

Tom's bid for political office began with an impressive 1,500-person announcement event on November 5, 1975, his 44th birthday, at the storied Gold Ballroom at the Hotel du Pont in Wilmington, Del. The *Philadelphia Inquirer* wrote of the event, "No one present could recall anything like it in the history of Wilmington political affairs. The crowded conditions seemed to highlight Evans' message — that togetherness will solve America's problems."[1]

Tom's announcement event at the Hotel du Pont in
Wilmington, Del. Present are John O'Hear, minister at
Christ Church, and Felix du Pont, among others.

The success of the event was no fluke. Tom
had been preparing for it throughout his career
and life, with active involvement in political,
business and social causes even before he stood
upon that stage. A copy of one of Tom's campaign
handouts highlights a man with varied connections
throughout Delaware and elsewhere. He
befriended Republicans and Democrats through
his moderate political stance and pragmatic

approach to problem solving. As to his affiliation, an article in *The Virginian-Pilot* quoted Tom saying, "I don't think I belong to any particular bloc. Having worked for Barry Goldwater and then having worked with Russ Peterson in Delaware, I got along reasonably well with both conservatives and liberals and never considered myself either one."[2] Even so, Tom ran as a Republican.

The campaign slogan was "I like Tom Evans" and son Rob wore it proudly. Along with Mary Page and Tom are their children, Page, Tommy and Rob.

Not surprisingly, Tom's campaign team included Democrats, Republicans and independents. Tom owed much of his big party turnout to a wonderful cadre of volunteers, including Patty Hobbs, Phyllis Wyeth, Tucker Rankin, Dr. Jim Beebe, Priscilla Rakestraw, and Laird and Peg Stabler, among many others.

The full force of his connections to date mobilized to elect the moderate Republican to succeed Pete du Pont, who won the bid for governor of Delaware in that year.

The years leading up to Tom's first run for office were full of discontent and disconnection in the country. Starting in the late '60s, urban riots and an unpopular war consumed the American psyche. As the new decade began, the nation faced Richard Nixon's indiscretions and impeachment and searched for a direction forward. Voters were looking for leaders to bring people together in contrast to the partisan bickering over Nixon's trial. Tom was that leader.

In November of 1976, although Delaware chose Democrat Jimmy Carter for president, Tom and Republican gubernatorial candidate Pete du Pont beat that trend. Tom narrowly defeated his

Democratic challenger Sam Shipley and took office in January of the following year. As with all his campaigns, Tom became friendly with those he ran against.

As a junior representative in the minority party, he knew he needed to endear himself to his colleagues. Tom had a lot of experience in politics through his involvement in the Republican National Committee and on Nixon's campaign team. Everyone knew who he was, but, since he hadn't worked personally with most of the other representatives, he had to build trust. Seasoned members of Congress didn't want the new guy to steal their thunder or undermine the work of the party. And so, he went to work.

"Polarized politics in Congress began in the 1970s and has been getting worse ever since," according to Pew Research Center.[3] As Tom stepped into office in 1977, the political divide deepened. Politicians began their march farther right and left in their respective parties, steeling their positions behind loyal party leaders. It was in this atmosphere that Tom, a moderate Republican, entered Congress. And, in that time, it was all the more critical to use conversation and compromise to gain support for difficult legislation from both sides of the aisle and foster bipartisanship among his colleagues.

For Tom, bipartisanship began at home. His wife, Mary Page, is unapologetically liberal and not afraid to go toe-to-toe with Tom on political matters. Often described as a straight shooter, she carries her petite frame with the confidence of a prizefighter. As Tom rose to the center of political influence and Mary Page grew in prominence in the art community, she wasn't content to play the role of the Congressman's wife. Especially not with Tom's Republican colleagues. And so, he worked to find "common ground."

For a time, their trajectories, along with their political and social priorities, propelled them in different directions. Common ground was sometimes hard to find.

At a small dinner party Frank Sinatra threw for Vice President Spiro Agnew, Mary Page spoke to Agnew about playing tennis earlier in the day with Hays Gorey, Washington correspondent for *Time* magazine. Vice President Spiro Agnew said, "You shouldn't play tennis with people like that."

Mary Page snapped back with finger wagging, "You shouldn't talk about people you don't know." Upon hearing her raised voice toward the vice president, his secret service crew descended upon her. She knew immediately she had made a mistake and remained uncharacteristically quiet for the rest of the evening. But she would have done it again, if given the chance.

It didn't stop there. In 1973, Tom's driver dropped Tom off at Nixon's second inaugural parade and proceeded to drop off Mary Page on another corner with the anti-Vietnam protesters. That evening, Tom hosted a party at the Watergate

Hotel in Washington to celebrate the victory with guests, including Senators Bob Dole and Chuck Percy. When the subject of Nixon's "Enemies List" came up in conversation, Mary Page expressed enthusiasm for the idea of being on it, as if it was a true badge of defiance. Then she was told, "You are." Whether she was officially on the list or in spirit, the divide Tom sought to bridge was clear.

Throughout his six years as a U.S. representative, he developed extensive contacts in Congress, the executive branch, throughout this country and in many countries around the world. He understood how personalities, varied interests, backgrounds and politics impacted the legislative process and leveraged that understanding to get people on his side. Whatever the legislation, cause or project, Tom engaged people and built broad-based coalitions to affect change.

Some of those conversations took place over rounds of golf. The winner of many amateur golf tournaments, Tom was no stranger to the links or the power of 18 holes to forge lasting friendships.

He teed off with congressmen, executives and influencers of all varieties.

As Tom eagerly awaited his committee assignments in his first term, he didn't leave it to chance. Tom used golf as a means to share his skills and interests with House leader Bob Michel. He secured posts on the Banking, Finance and Urban Affairs Committee and the Merchant Marine and Fisheries Committee, where he would go on to make lasting impacts on the causes he championed.

During his time in Congress, Tom became captain of the Republican Golf Team. They played the Democrats once a year at The Courses at Andrews in Washington, D.C., for a rousing 36 holes. Through golf he made friends from both sides of the aisle, including Marty Russo, captain of the Democrats' team, and Speaker of the House Tip O'Neill. Despite his competitive nature, he knew when to slice one into the rough so as not to outshine his golf partner.

Golf, along with countless meals and drinks, became the water cooler around which Tom forged friendships. As much as he focused on the technical or historical background required to write and support each piece of legislation, Tom also worked to nurture relationships. He needed each relationship in the legislative battles he faced over the next six years in Congress to accomplish great things for the environment, the country and countries around the world. His colleagues needed him, too.

CHAPTER FOUR

LEGISLATIVE VICTORIES

Tom's committee assignments, Merchant Marine and Fisheries Committee and the Committee on Banking, Finance and Urban Affairs, offered platforms to support and forward issues of importance. And he wasted no time.

Prior to his focus on the environment, he got to work early in his tenure focusing on legislative process as his first session began. As a member of Banking, Finance and Urban Affairs, Tom pushed for public transparency on committee votes nearly before his seat was warm. The rule change required publication of each committee member's vote and whether it was cast in person or by proxy.[4]

It demonstrated his willingness to speak up for good government policies, even as a new congressman. The majority party, Democrats at the time, often opposes transparency in government as fiercely as it is favored by the minority party, so it required his adept skills of gathering support from both sides of the aisle to get it passed.

Also, within the Banking Committee, Tom was appointed to the Subcommittee on Housing, where, among other things, he influenced funding for housing for the middle class and poor. He gained support in his home state from Democrats and Republicans for championing the Quaker Hill Development in Wilmington in the late 1970s, earning praise from Mayor Bill McLaughlin and the Rev. Otis Herring, a pastor from a well-attended church in downtown Wilmington. Both became good friends and strong supporters.

In his role as the head of economic development earlier in the decade, he connected with leaders and citizens to promote business and job growth in Delaware's largest city. He was pleased to continue support through the affordable housing project. Constituents, in turn, supported him.

The unveiling of the Quaker Hill Development plan in Wilmington, Del., in 1979 with Mayor Bill McLaughlin, State Senator Herman Holloway and others.

His work on the committee continued with world-changing legislation. Along with bills to support the World Bank Regional Development Project and aid for countries, including Sudan and Jamaica, Tom ushered through a provision that was a contributing factor to ending apartheid. Many wanted to end all assistance to South Africa due to the rising public outcry against the ruling white minority. Tom felt this would only hurt the very people our country wanted to assist — the oppressed Blacks in South Africa. Instead, Tom joined fellow Banking Committeeman, Paul Tsongas from Massachusetts (later a U.S. senator and presidential candidate), in authoring the Evans-Tsongas amendment that made export-import assistance and loans conditional on treating people fairly. By guaranteeing loans with U.S. trading partners through the Export-Import Bank, the legislation forced the hands of the white ruling class and, in turn, changed the course of history.[5]

After the amendment passed, Tom received praise from William Raspberry in an opinion article in the *Washington Post* for his stance on the amendment. He also received long-lasting gratitude from the aforementioned Rev. Leon Sullivan, founder of the OIC and long-time board member of General Motors (the first Black man to be appointed to the board of a major corporation). GM was the largest employer in South Africa at the time. As an anti-apartheid activist, he created the

Sullivan Principles, a code of conduct to guide companies operating in South Africa, in 1977. In his book, *Moving Mountains*, Sullivan penned a personal inscription to Tom:

> *To Tom Evans — whose insight and actions in the U.S. Congress helped to lead to the ending of apartheid in South Africa and the freeing of a nation. I am grateful to you for all you do to help others.*
>
> *~ Leon Sullivan*

Although apartheid didn't end until years later, it remained one of the initiatives of which Tom was most proud. He, along with Rep. Tsongas, provided leadership on the amendment. It's an accomplishment he shares with many others who supported it.[6]

CHAPTER FIVE

STATE OF THE ENVIRONMENT

To set the stage for the environmental legislation on which Tom was about to embark, it's important to place it firmly within the framework of the time. It was a tumultuous period in society as well as in politics. But the post-industrialized country had ignored the cries of environmentalists and the environment for far too long.

An environmental crisis came to a head during the 1960s. Toxic leaded gas, tenuous nuclear power plants, unchecked air pollution, nuclear waste dumping, coal ash accidents and more plagued the United States and the world. It was during this time that Cleveland's Cuyahoga River caught fire, to the bewilderment of the city residents despite their having become accustomed to the pollution as an unavoidable side effect of economic stability. The sentiment was echoed in cities and throughout the country. The land was ravaged for oil or otherwise developed beyond capacity to fill the coffers of the few at a cost paid in human health, as well as the welfare of wildlife.[7]

Fortunately, defenders of the environment organized and spoke out. Early in the decade, environmental activist Rachel Carson led the way by highlighting the dangers of pollution and toxic chemicals and the link between public health and the environment in her widely popular book, *Silent Spring*. As the decade wore on, The World Wildlife Fund was founded, along with the Environmental Defense Fund and Greenpeace.[8]

Environmental groups and corporate polluters continued to battle in a protracted tug of war into the 1970s. Major initiatives in the '60s and early into the '70s seemed to have tilted in favor of people over profits in both the non-profit sector and federal regulation.

Chief among these initiatives was the first Earth Day in 1970, organized by Sen. Gaylord Nelson of Wisconsin. It "would come to provide a voice to this emerging environmental consciousness, channeling the energy of the anti-war protest movement to put environmental concerns on the front page."[9] Once in the public sphere, mounting pressure hit Washington.

By the time Richard Nixon took office, the drumbeats of change were evident. With increasing pressure from the public and deteriorating conditions in all areas of the environment, President Nixon initiated a groundbreaking 37-point plan, eventually resulting in the historic decision to create the Environmental Protection Agency (EPA). Its purpose was to oversee and implement the newly passed Clean Air Act, among other initiatives. The Clean Water Act was soon to follow.[10, 11]

Despite progress in some areas, there was still more to do. Incidents like the one in 1978 in

Love Canal, a community near Niagara Falls, came into the spotlight as a decades-old chemical waste site percolated up into homes and schools, causing illness and disease, along with millions of taxpayer dollars spent evacuating the families and mitigating the damage. It was just one of the stories that sparked continued societal ire. For decades, the government had turned its back on protecting the environment and the health of its citizens.[12]

With his history of environmental interest, Tom's place on the Merchant Marine and Fisheries Committee seemed fated. He was ushered into office at a time when society was ready for action on the environment, even if political will lagged behind.

CHAPTER SIX

THE CASE AGAINST SLUDGE

D espite being a junior member of a minority party and the only congressman from his state, Tom went to work early on the Merchant Marine and Fisheries Committee (later called the Resources Committee). Also, early into his first session, he befriended fellow committee member Bill Hughes, a Democrat from South Jersey. They teamed up for what would be Tom's first major legislative achievement.

In 1977, Hughes and Evans worked on an amendment, originally authored by Hughes in 1975, to the Ocean Dumping Act (officially called the Marine Protection, Research and Sanctuaries Act of 1972). Its purpose was to regulate ocean dumping of sewage sludge off the Delaware, New

Jersey and Maryland coasts from New York City and other municipalities in the Mid-Atlantic.

It also "prohibits the Administrator of the Environmental Protection Agency, after December 31, 1981, from issuing or renewing any permit which authorizes the dumping of sewage sludge in ocean waters."[13]

A General Accounting Office memo to the chair of the Merchant Marine and Fisheries Committee in the Subcommittee on Oceanography said, in part, "Sludge dumping is not the only source, or even the most significant source, of marine pollution. In the New York Bight, for example, more than 7 million wet tons of dredged material were dumped in 1978 at a site only seven miles from shore. Further, 500 million gallons of raw sewage are discharged to the area each day by New York City" and others.[14]

Despite 1972 legislation calling for the ban, little progress had been made by the EPA to halt the dumping or even to slow its use to date. Pressure mounted on the EPA from the municipal dumpers to delay implementation of the law. The EPA found itself waffling on enacting it, and an amendment was offered to bolster the original bill and force the EPA to act.[15]

As a summer resident of the seaside town of Rehoboth Beach, Delaware, and an avid fisherman, Tom was naturally concerned and jumped in to help pass the legislation. The presence of sewage sludge along the Mid-Atlantic coast could destroy the environment for wildlife, jobs and revenue for the beach communities, and also tarnish the bucolic beaches of his beloved state for himself and his constituents. The two men represented the states most severely impacted by the sludge and were the natural torchbearers of the bill.

Unfortunately, the Chair of the Merchant Marine and Fisheries Committee, John Murphy, a Democrat from Staten Island, strongly opposed any effort to halt the dumping, as did many other committee members. The opposition from New York City and other municipalities was a monumental hurdle to gathering support.

Despite a challenge from the chair, Tom's cohort from New Jersey introduced the amendment to the Ocean Dumping Act to end sewage sludge dumping by their neighbors to the north, and it was "pushed vigorously by Evans," according to *The Morning News* in Wilmington.[16] To bolster the effort, he got support from Pete McCloskey, the ranking Republican on the committee. McCloskey was a proud Marine and enamored with Tom's relative, Lewis "Chesty" Puller, Lieutenant General in the Marine Corps. Puller was "the most decorated Marine in history, and the only Marine to receive five Navy Crosses."[17]

Tom perceptively used the connection and made McCloskey an ally in the battle.

The Morning News wrote, "Evans, who had spent more than two hours on the phone Tuesday night seeking support from committee members, showed up at yesterday's meeting with proxies from six members who expected to be absent."

In Tom's signature bipartisan effort, the prominent and second-ranking Democrat on the committee, Thomas Ludlow Ashley of Ohio, gave Tom his proxy during the bill's markup, where final details of proposed legislation are determined. When asked why an influential Democrat would extend such a show of support to a junior member of the opposing party, Tom remarked, "Sometimes, you just have to ask. And, we had many mutual friends."

"As yesterday's debate was in progress, Evans met in a corridor outside the committee room with Rep. Joel Pritchard, R-Wash., who was still on the fence. Evans and an aide spent 10 minutes trying to persuade Pritchard and an aide to support the ban. Pritchard eventually voted, 'yes'."[18]

With pressure from Hughes, McCloskey, Tom and other members of the committee, the chair relented and allowed a vote. It was voted out of committee and was signed into law in the spring of 1977 by President Jimmy Carter, despite not having support from the chair.

As his late former aide Darry Carmine put it, within months of his election, "Tom quickly became something of a master at bringing together members with widely divergent politics to accomplish something important to the nation. I was amazed to see liberals join with conservative forerunners of the tea party to support legislation I suspected they would never have supported without Tom serving as a catalyst."[19]

His efforts to work across the aisle to get things done got people's attention. The achievement solidified allies on the committee for his next challenge — defending the vast wilderness of Alaska.

CHAPTER SEVEN

SAVING ALASKA'S WILDERNESS

After Tom's work on the sludge issue, he became deeply involved in a massive environmental legislative effort — the Alaska National Interest Lands Conservation Act (ANILCA). The bill was more familiarly named the Alaska Lands Act.

Democrat Mo Udall of Arizona authored the bill in 1978. As the chair of the House Interior and Insular Affairs Committee, Udall sought out Tom to bridge the partisan divide and sign on as an early co-sponsor of the legislation. Tom's reputation for working across the aisle and adeptness at rallying widespread support made him an asset to the cause.

Mo Udall succeeded his brother Stewart Udall as a representative from Arizona's second district when Stewart took the position of secretary of the Interior. Mo, the younger Udall, carried the tradition of environmental stewardship into his congressional seat. As a 1976 presidential candidate, Mo came off his losing bid with fierce determination. Mo and Tom, along with an impressive list of congressional backers, got to work on legislation that was years in the making.

Due to a provision in earlier legislation, a looming deadline to enact this bill created urgency and energy. As a precursor and catalyst for the bill, the Alaska Native Claims Settlement Act of 1971 (ANCSA) was signed into law by President Nixon. The bill not only settled claims and clarified interests of the native Alaskans after statehood in 1958, but also set aside millions of acres of land for withdrawal from development. The caveat to the legislation was that the secretary of the Interior had to withdraw the lands within nine months of its passage, and Congress was required to act within five years to seal protection for the withdrawn lands, or they would be released and open for development.

In 1972, Interior Secretary Rogers Morton withdrew 127,000,000 acres of land for protection. It was up to Congress to make the protection permanent. The first bill introduced to complete the provisions laid out in ANCSA followed in 1973. The bill, and many to follow, were defeated in Congress due to lobbying by development and oil interests in the state. Finally, in 1978, H.B. 39, the Alaska National Interest Lands Conservation Act, was introduced in the House by Mo Udall.[20]

In an effort to fully appreciate the impact of the bill, Tom packed his bags for Alaska. From Seattle to Anchorage to Fairbanks, he flew in comfortable commercial carriers. But to really experience the vast wilderness of Alaska, Tom boarded a small prop plane, dwarfed by the massive expanse of what he witnessed below. Under the careful operation of a bush pilot, Tom took his seat as co-pilot, leaving any thoughts of the creature comforts of Wilmington or Washington behind — no staff, restaurants or phone service. They headed north toward the Arctic Circle and the Arctic National Wildlife

Refuge, land preserved by the Wilderness Act of 1964 that was signed into law by President Johnson. ANILCA sought to expand significantly the lands included in the refuge, among other provisions.

In an experience that Tom described as awe-inspiring, they saw rivers and streams so pristine you could drink from them, many filled with a plethora of salmon while also witnessing polar bears caring for their cubs. They flew over land where, just months before, caribou migrated by the thousands from winter homes in other areas in Alaska or Canada for an annual trek of up to 2,700 miles to calve their young. After feeding in the lush plains, they return home at the end of the summer — this time with calves in tow.[21]

Ill-prepared for a late-July snowstorm, their trip was cut short. Nonetheless, before Tom left for home, he met with stakeholders from both sides, seeking to understand the urgency and drawbacks of the proposed legislation. Despite the shortened trip, the experience left Tom more committed than ever to preserve the wilderness for its native inhabitants and for generations to come, even if it meant facing powerful lobbyists back in Washington.

Standing in opposition to the bill were big oil, the National Rifle Association and a cadre of Alaska residents. Sen. Ted Stevens, a Republican from Alaska, was instrumental in weakening the 1978 bill, which eventually led to its initial defeat. The two years between introducing the bill and its passage were plagued with emotional ups and downs. Passage often seemed imminent only to be undermined by one legislator or another.

Without passage of ANILCA and with protections about to expire for much of the Alaska wilderness withdrawn through ANCSA, President Jimmy Carter was compelled to use the Antiquities Act to designate large areas in Alaska as national monuments. The Antiquities Act was originally passed in 1906, enabling presidential power to protect native artifacts and lands of national or cultural interest. The use of the Antiquities Act gave way to the passage of a more comprehensive bill in 1980, but not without a fight.

Although the bill had many co-sponsors and advocates, Udall sought out Tom for tactical assistance. Speaker Tip O'Neill, a close ally of Udall and often described as a fierce partisan, nonetheless offered his private dining room to the duo for meetings out of earshot or eyesight of detractors. They discussed which legislators needed some kind of compromise and who would be the best messenger to make the deal. Meetings often lasted for hours and continued for months. No staff or other legislators participated to ensure the privacy of each conversation.

Despite progress made by Udall, Tom and others, the political tides turned once more after the 1980 election. With years of debate and compromise behind them, Udall and his supporters pushed through an imperfect bill to head off a threat from a more conservative Congress to weaken the bill further. Tom took the reins as the Republican floor leader for the Alaska

Lands Act in 1980 and oversaw its eventual passage. He stressed the importance of wildlife and the interconnectedness of our existence. He passionately spoke to fellow representatives on the House floor: "Wildlife cannot speak, so it's our responsibility to speak for them."

Although supporters pushed for a more robust bill, conservationists cheered the outcome. In its final form, "The Alaska National Interest Lands Conservation Act of 1980 provided for 43,585,000 acres of new national parklands in Alaska and the addition of 53,720,000 acres to the National Wildlife Refuge System," among other notable conservation designations.[22]

In a post-election article in 1980 in *The Evening Journal* of Wilmington, Tom says he "considers the [Alaska Lands Act] legislation a proper balance of development interest with environmental concerns — like critical habitat needs of wildlife." Responsible compromise is a familiar refrain from the congressman.[23]

In a 2002 speech at the University of Delaware, Tom reflected on the legislative victory.

"This landmark piece of legislation set aside additional millions of acres of land and designated them as wilderness areas. It was a gigantic effort to achieve the preservation of some irreplaceable, pristine areas of wilderness for us and for future generations. I was honored to have been one of the three principal congressional backers and the Republican floor leader for the bill.

"The bill passed, and millions of acres of land were protected, but there was something else equally important. There was a tremendous lobbying effort against it and millions of dollars were spent. The dollars spent by our Alaska Coalition paled in comparison to the lobbying effort that attempted to prevent passage of the legislation that was to protect wild scenic rivers, wetlands, polar bears, songbirds, caribou, ducks and other wildlife of every description.

"We won with 60-plus Republicans voting yes. It was, indeed, a truly bipartisan effort; and that, unfortunately, does not take place very often in today's political climate.

"Afterward, three of us were invited to a very emotional victory celebration hosted by the Alaska Coalition. That coalition consisted primarily of young people who spent the summer in Washington. They came to Washington to protect a great treasure for the future. John Seiberling of Ohio, who chaired the principal subcommittee having jurisdiction over this issue, and Mo Udall, a dedicated environmentalist from Arizona, and I were deeply touched by their invitation, and the warm reception we received. I believe I can safely say it was certainly one of the best invitations I've received in my lifetime.

"Mo Udall and John Seiberling both spoke eloquently and certainly covered the importance of the legislation. I didn't want to repeat them, so I took a slightly different tack and said that victory today was great in terms of conservation and preservation of millions of pristine acres. But there was an equally important victory today — all of you proved that regardless of dollars and political pressure, our constitutional system of government works. You can still win, and that's the American way."

In February of that year, Rep. Robert Andrews (D-N.J.) entered this speech into the congressional record to bolster support for the continued protection of the precious Alaska wilderness.

On the 25th anniversary of the passage of the Alaska Lands Act, the Alaska Wilderness League celebrated with a weekend of events in Anchorage. President Jimmy Carter gave the keynote speech on Saturday, while Tom was honored to deliver a keynote the following day. His speech focused on the vigilance needed to protect Alaska's wilderness amidst constant pressure to destroy it for monetary gain.

Once this fight ended, Tom prepared for his next challenge — shoring up America's coastline.

CHAPTER EIGHT

DO IT ON YOUR OWN NICKEL

Through Tom's work on previous coastal issues under Gov. Russ Peterson's Task Force on Marine and Coastal Affairs nearly a decade before, he recognized the urgent need to act to protect the fragile coastline of the country. Failure to do so could impact the habitat for a variety of wildlife, as well as the protective barrier against strong storms.

Many attempts failed to pass coastline-protecting bills for 20-30 years. No bill had ever come to a vote in any committee, let alone a full vote of the House or Senate. There was no political courage to stand up to powerful interest groups, like oil conglomerates and commercial developers, regardless of the cost to taxpayers, destruction of wildlife habitats, or harm to life and property in the hands of increasingly powerful storms.

Into his second term, Tom led the way to the first step toward protecting the U.S. coastline. In an effort to make headway towards the eventual passage of a more expansive bill, he offered an amendment to the Omnibus Budget Reconciliation Act in 1981, along with Rep. Fernand St Germain (D-R.I.), chair of the Banking Committee. The Financial Services Subcommittee on Housing, Community Development and Insurance held jurisdiction over the National Flood Insurance Program enacted in 1968 to provide flood insurance in storm-prone regions to homeowners. The presence of insurance provided needed protection for individuals and businesses, but also an incentive for property developers to build regardless of the risk in an area.

From the onset of his time on the committee, Tom positioned himself alongside St Germain. Frequent dinners together to discuss the day's important and not-so-important issues helped him gain friendship and support from an influential leader across the aisle. Representatives of the nation's two smallest states (among others) teamed up to protect their coastlines and economies on which environmental stability depended.

The provision, known as the Evans-St Germain Amendment, prohibited the issuance of new federal flood insurance subsidies for properties in undeveloped barrier islands. It also covered any substantial improvement of structures located on the land. The amendment was to have a significant impact on the way disaster relief was funded and effectively altered the behavior of would-be developers.

The amendment directed the Department of the Interior to develop maps identifying storm-prone areas along the Atlantic and Gulf Coasts that should be protected. At first, the Interior, headed by a slightly reluctant James Watt, was a little slow in creating the maps. The reluctance was eventually overcome when Tom reached out to

President Reagan, who got a commitment from the secretary to give Tom whatever he needed.

This provision only eliminated federal flood insurance, but it was the forerunner of the Coastal Barrier Resources Act, the landmark legislation Tom would champion in the coming year. It did nothing directly to stop development but put up a significant obstacle to developing fragile lands. The amendment was part of a nationwide movement toward thoughtful environmental policy that followed more than a decade of environmental consciousness and public outrage.

Years later, Tom wrote his justification for this legislation and continued protection of our coast. "For centuries, mankind has had a fascination with the sea. In America, that fascination has become an obsession generating a frenzy to acquire and build second and third homes on fragile oceanfront property. Americans, mostly wealthy ones, are today fiercely searching for building sites on coastal land that is fast becoming so scarce that people feel compelled to take on the inevitable forces of nature by building in environmentally sensitive, storm-prone areas.

"Incredibly, our federal government is encouraging high-risk coastal development by, among other things, subsidizing the cost of storm damage insurance. The availability of federal insurance at bargain-basement prices through the National Flood Insurance Program is usually the key factor in determining whether a developer will build a vacation castle in a storm-prone area.

"The most sensitive areas of our coastline are the thousands of low-lying barrier islands found mostly along the Atlantic and Gulf Coasts. These islands are the mainland's first line of defense against the full fury of storms and hurricanes. They also create and sustain, among other things, the estuaries that nurture fish stocks and other marine life so important for recreational and commercial fishing and protect other natural habitats, including nesting areas and spawning grounds."[24]

With that passion, Tom fought his battles for the environment. The amendment passed in 1981.

CHAPTER NINE

PROTECTING THE BARRIERS

T here was one motto that reverberated through the halls of Congress and in meetings with environmental activists and pro-industry, pro-development advocates.

"Do it on your own nickel and not on the American taxpayers."

It was the basis for the Evans-St Germain Amendment in the Omnibus Budget Reconciliation Act in the Banking Committee, and the foundation for gaining support for the eventual Coastal Barrier Resources Act.

Tom reached out to a natural ally in the Senate — Sen. John Chafee, a Republican from Rhode Island and chair of the subcommittee in Marine Resources, the Senate's sister committee to the House's Merchant Marine and Fisheries

Committee, of which Tom was a member. His work with fellow statesman Rep. St Germain of Rhode Island on the Omnibus bill only strengthened the bond.

In developing the bill, Evans and Chafee kept three things in mind: 1) to minimize the loss of human life by discouraging development in high-risk areas vulnerable to storm surges and hurricane winds; 2) to reduce wasteful expenditure of federal resources; and 3) to protect the natural resources associated with undeveloped coastal barriers.[25]

In addressing the first point, development along coastal barriers meant more people in harm's way during increasingly powerful storms. More human inhabitants made it increasingly difficult to evacuate in dire situations and increased stress on emergency management of the area.

In 2014, during one of many testimonies before Congress, Tom summed up the vital purpose of the coastal barriers. "The barrier lands are the first line of defense for the mainland against the force of hurricanes and other strong storms. They create and maintain, among other things, the estuaries that nurture fish stocks so crucial for recreational and commercial fishing. These lands provide natural habitats for numerous species of birds and other wildlife, including federally endangered species. The wetlands that barrier lands protect are vital in many ways. In addition to being spawning grounds for fish and shellfish of all varieties, they also serve as an essential element in flood control and pollution reduction, especially in the event of a storm."

Tom stood steadfast with his belief that our nation's barrier lands were resources that should be preserved and not exploited. This belief was, and is, especially true in coastal states where tourism is so important to their economies. While there may be short-term monetary gains to be had by developing along the most fragile parts of the coastline, the value of barrier lands to the environment is priceless.

But the environment wasn't the only target of the bill. To appeal to fiscal hawks in Congress, the bill addressed the aftermath of storms. Property and infrastructure on barrier islands are often the first to succumb to storm surges and hurricane-force winds. After nature speaks her mind, federal dollars pour in to rebuild and restore what was in her path.

The previous year, the Evans-St Germain Amendment had eliminated the National Flood Insurance program for designated coastal areas. The Coastal Barrier Resources Act expanded on the idea with the elimination of an additional 52 federal subsidies targeted at infrastructure. Unlike the National Flood Insurance Program that provides an insurance pool for personal and business properties, CBRA also sought to eliminate funding for the rebuilding of roads, bridges, lighting, electric grids and the like. In a popular free-market approach, the bill did nothing to stop developers from developing the land. It merely took away all incentives to do so. As Tom often said, "it ended welfare for the wealthy and got taxpayers off the hook."

In addition, the bill established the Coastal Barrier Resources System, to be managed by the Department of the Interior. The department was charged with creating the maps and maintaining the integrity of the system. The Evans-St Germain Amendment laid the groundwork the previous year requiring the development of coastal maps used to enforce the law.

Despite being opposed by the oil industry, real estate developers and other pro-business lobbyists, Chafee and Evans introduced the Coastal Barrier Resources Act in both chambers in April 1981. Like numerous prior attempts at coastal land preservation, no one gave it a chance of passage.

On the way to Washington, D.C., from his home state of Rhode Island, Sen. Chafee agreed to hold a joint news conference with Evans in Wilmington, Del., in front of a small crowd of supporters and members of the media. It was one of many efforts to gain support locally, although it would take a virtual army to make headway nationwide.

Tom with Sen. John Chafee of Rhode Island at the senator's office, showcasing the proposed CBRA maps.

Tom was up for the challenge. He knew the key to success was to include as many people as possible in the process. With an excellent reputation for integrity and honesty, he set out to gather opinions and support from disparate constituencies, especially members of Congress. Central to the plan was his gift for listening, understanding various positions and, most important, a knack for finding acceptable middle ground. The next 18 months would prove the most challenging and, ultimately, the most rewarding.

CHAPTER TEN

THE COALITION

B etween April 1981 and October 1982, Tom stood with others in a protracted battle to protect the future of the coast. Opposition to the bill was varied and well-funded. Chief among the opponents were the real estate agents, land developers, big oil and a phalanx of lawyer lobbyists.

As with many environmental regulations, the main objection of industry groups centered on economics. Historically, the drive for profits eclipsed any public or environmental good, like the unfettered capitalism of Niagara Falls in the 1800s that virtually destroyed the area in search of a quick buck. This proposed bill proved no exception. Deep pockets for lawyers and lobbyists, along with unrestrained campaign contributions to key representatives, pressured fault lines in the House. Lobbyists had taken down earlier efforts to protect the coast and threatened the Coastal Barrier Resources Act as well.

In 1981, Democrats controlled the U.S. House of Representatives. Evans was a junior member of a very minority party at the time. John Sweeney of *The News Journal* wrote, "In his era, Republicans in that body were generally viewed by long-reigning Democrats more like a comfortable piece of furniture than a force to be reckoned with."[26] With a Republican-held majority in the Senate, the real fight was in the House. It required Tom to gain support not only from his fellow Republicans, but from Democrats as well.

Once the bill was introduced in April of 1981, it was assigned to the Merchant Marine and Fisheries Committee, and landed in the Subcommittee on Fisheries and Wildlife Conservation and the Environment. Rep. John Breaux (D-La.), Chairman of the committee, said he "couldn't offer Tom a hearing at this time."

Undaunted, Tom set out to form a coalition of support for the bill that was so remarkable and varied, lawmakers from both parties would have to take notice. And so, the work began.

Tom's work ethic and passion for the cause meant he would lead the effort. He did most of the initial bill-writing himself, with input from staff and likely supporters. As the process began, he worked with his staff sending op-eds to newspapers around the country and crafting speeches to anyone who would listen. His staff reached out to other Congressional staff, while Tom concentrated his efforts on other members. Without the benefit of 24-hour media or viral videos, he nonetheless pursued the mission with persistence.

Tom relentlessly made phone calls and talked to everyone on the committee. Over lunch, dinner, golf, drinks, or a meeting in their office, he offered an honest conversation about the legislation that he promoted as making "eminently good sense." During this time, he talked personally to well over 100 members of Congress, along with many others.

Through his work on other legislation, like the Ocean Dumping Act, he already had the support of committee members Bill Hughes and Pete McCloskey. He looked not just for support, but for each representative to buy into the bill. He lined up co-sponsors and gave legislators every opportunity to have a say in the legislation so that each member personally felt they had a hand in its success.

Support also came from a small cohort in his weekly prayer group — Don Bonker, a Democrat from Washington, Bill Nelson, Democrat from Florida and later a senator, and his cousin, Paul Trible, Republican from Virginia, also later a senator. In his book, *A Higher Calling*, Bonker recounts the beginnings of the group. The vision was to "get people whose politics were different to not only sit together, but to eat together, talk and to ultimately realize that even when we were driven by opposing points of view, we could also be unified in our love for each other and for what just might be best for the world."[27] It made their politics a place filled with much-needed humanity. Tom cherished their small community. Although the group often voted differently, their commitment to each other lasted well past their years in Congress. On this issue, Tom had them by his side.

Tom's weekly prayer group meeting with Paul Trible, Don Bonker and Bill Nelson.

Other early supporters included Ed Markey, Ileana Ros-Lehtinen, Steny Hoyer and House Minority leader Bob Michel. It would take more than just congressional support to move John Breaux, chair of the subcommittee in which the fledgling bill was placed, to hold hearings. So Tom searched for support outside of the walls of Congress.

He first established an unprecedented coalition of environmentalists. National and local conservancies, like the National Wildlife Federation, coastal wildlife advocates, land management experts, sportsmen, crabbers and fishermen, among many others.

One of the most ardent advocates was Americans for the Coast, a group established by Larry Rockefeller, that included about 100 of America's most well-known leaders from various fields of interest. Members of the group ranged from celebrated artist Jamie Wyeth to the diplomat Henry Kissinger. These and other prominent contributors, like William F. Buckley, Jacqueline Kennedy Onassis and Anne Morrow Lindbergh, pledged their support in some way and lent credibility to the policy. Rockefeller later wrote to

Tom, "There would be no bill today had you not been so deeply interested and made such an active, lasting and creative commitment."

With the balanced wisdom in the bill, fiscal hawks jumped on board. Taxpayers for Commonsense robustly carried the banner for conservatives, placing it directly at odds with the traditionally pro-business interests of the Republican party. Nonetheless, the federal taxpayers' savings from the measure gave political shelter to those who might otherwise have cowered.

Then there was the mighty American Red Cross. The mission statement taken from their website reads: "The American Red Cross prevents and alleviates human suffering in the face of emergencies by mobilizing the power of volunteers and the generosity of donors." The Coastal Barrier Resources Act prevented or decreased the necessity for their emergency assistance in the aftermath of a storm. Their impact and influence on the cause were notable. When they asked

Breaux to hold a hearing, it was hard for him to say no.

All in all, approximately 35 editorials in a number of the country's major newspapers proved to tip support in favor of the bill. In particular, a favorable editorial in the *New Orleans Picayune*, Breaux's hometown newspaper, became a turning point. Although Breaux didn't support the bill, he was unwilling to withstand the pressure. He finally relented and allowed a hearing.

But the fight was far from over. Despite growing support, the opposition arrived in force. Tom encouraged media coverage to keep discussion in the public eye and hold committee members accountable. Tom and his broad coalition stood firm in the face of highly paid lobbyists and lawyers from the National Homebuilders Association, the National Association of Realtors and big oil companies. He encouraged friends on the committee to ask questions and give remarks that Tom prepared for them. A consistent message rang throughout the hearing: "we shouldn't be playing Russian roulette with American taxpayers' dollars."

At the close of the hearing, there was still work to do. Although it was voted out of committee, details of the bill and specific lands designated for inclusion were disputed by various legislators. Tom made it his mission to listen to each one of those opposing the legislation — really listen. Trent Lott felt the heat from pro-building groups about protection of barrier lands along the Mississippi coast. It came down to one mile of value to both sides. Tom suggested the release of one-quarter mile of coast out of the protected maps as a compromise. Lott agreed and then supported the bill. This scene played out over and over until the final vote on the House floor.

In the end, the Coastal Barrier Resources Act was ultimately crafted by wide-ranging and diverse interests — Republicans and Democrats, conservatives and liberals, environmentalists and tax hawks. This willingness to work together existed because the concepts embodied in CBRA made eminently good sense then, as they do today. William Raspberry, in his *Washington Post* column, called it "common-sense legislation."

A *Delaware Business Times* article by Kathy Canavan, author of *Lincoln's Final Hours*, noted, "Earlier attempts to save the coastline belly-flopped. Slowly and steadily, Chaffee and Evans formed a coalition of disparate groups and focused on their individual sweet spots — the Red Cross hoping to save lives, the Taxpayer's Union hoping to save money, hunters, fishermen and conservation groups hoping to save fragile lands."[28]

As Tom would later say of the Act, "Support for environmental protection, fiscal restraint and saving lives cannot and should not be partisan issues. CBRA was supported by those with wide-ranging philosophies. It was a marvelous example of our democratic system of government working in the best interests of our country."

But one of Tom's most important relationships began a few years earlier. In 1976, as a national delegate to the Republican convention, he threw his support behind President Gerald Ford, eschewing Ronald Reagan for the presidential nomination. Although he liked Reagan, as a national committeeman, he felt backing the incumbent president was best for the party and the country at the time. Ford went on to win the Republican nomination but was narrowly defeated by Jimmy Carter for president that year.

Tom with President Gerald Ford at the Republican National Convention in Kansas City in 1976. Tom gave a seconding speech for Ford that year.

After the election, with spiraling inflation, rising unemployment and an energy crisis underway, Tom knew the country needed a new direction. Feeling badly for the loss in the previous election, he threw himself into Ronald Reagan's 1980 campaign in typical Tom Evans fashion. At a Chowder and Marching Club dinner, a hide-in-plain-sight secret Republican organization, he vowed his support to the California governor.[29]

Tom pledging his support to Gov. Reagan for the Republican nomination at a Chowder and Marching Club anniversary dinner.

As a previous candidate for president and a popular California governor, Reagan already had a strong base of support. His narrow loss for the 1976 nomination behind the incumbent president demonstrated his popularity and the electorate's hunger for sweeping changes in a beleaguered nation.

Tom established the CORE Group made up of Republican members of the House who were early supporters of Reagan. The sole purpose of the group was to ensure Reagan won the Republican nomination, and they were active on behalf of the governor. Although there were several candidates vying for the nod to head the Republican ticket, CIA Director George H.W. Bush proved to be his only real competition in the race.

Tom called upon his extensive contacts in Congress and elsewhere. He encouraged the various constituencies to vote for Reagan in the Republican primary and to publicly throw their support behind the governor.

To bolster the impact of the CORE group, Tom announced the meetings to the media. He insisted that Reagan meet with fellow House members, not just the senators, and the coverage enhanced the effort.

Tom is seated next to President Reagan at a CORE Group meeting. Present at the meeting are Carroll Campbell, Dick Schulze, Mickey Edwards, Henry Hyde, Jim Baker, Ken Duberstein, M.B. Oglesby, Lee Atwater and Trent Lott.

Although Bush remained in the race until June of 1980, the understated CIA Director and moderate Republican succumbed to the charming actor turned politician. Once Bush dropped out of the race, Tom immediately called the Bush camp, asked for his backing and got his public support.

Once Ronald Reagan secured the nomination, energy switched to the general election. By mid-1980, Tom was chairman of the Congressional Campaign Committee for Reagan. When campaign chairman John Sears was fired, Tom's role increased. His extensive connections and work ethic made him a valuable asset to Reagan and the campaign team.

After Gov. Reagan secured the Republican nomination,
Tom asks for George Bush's public support for Reagan.

He also became a member of the executive committee of the Reagan-Bush campaign. Tom met with the top political minds in the business. At that time, Sen. Paul Laxalt (R-Nev.), Reagan's campaign chairman, described Evans as a "sound, commonsense Republican who provides some balance to the conservatism usually associated with the Reagan philosophy." Laxalt goes on to say, "His role is now beyond that of just an adviser. He is an invaluable, upfront guy with a minimum of ego."[30]

Because of his dedication, Tom enjoyed the honor of introducing Gov. Reagan in September 1980 in front of 22,000 people outside the Capitol.

Tom introducing Ronald Reagan at the Capitol.

Gov. Reagan speaking after Tom's introduction. Behind Reagan are Tom, a member of the Secret Service, George H.W. Bush, Howard Baker, John Rhodes and Bob Michel.

He also gave the key seconding speech at the Republican convention that year. According to reporting, he energized the crowd and brought the delegates to their feet. "Ronald Reagan can rekindle the spark that made America great. With our help and with the help of millions of Americans just like us, the party will grow into a roaring fire that will light the beacon once again and tell the world that America is back to stay."[31]

Reagan's "Kitchen Cabinet" was established in California when he was governor. The Kitchen Cabinet included a group of his closest advisors to provide unfiltered counsel and advice to the governor, then presidential candidate, and eventually president.

The 1980 election brought a landslide re-election victory for Tom and a big win for Republicans, with Reagan taking the White House. Will Wilson, a member of Reagan's original Kitchen Cabinet, interviewed people for the president's official federal cabinet positions. During Tom's brief tenure as part of the Kitchen Cabinet, he was invited to help with interviews for the various posts. Their charge was to find strong supporters of Reagan, astute political minds, substantial experience and demonstrated campaign advocates. Loyalty to Reagan was an important factor.

Unwavering support sealed lasting gratitude with the newly elected President Reagan along with key individuals like Ed Meese, Drew Lewis and Richard Allen in the years to come. Tom had the president's ear on issues of importance — like the Coastal Barrier Resources Act. An associate of Tom's noted in a Wilmington *Evening Journal* article, "We now have the most powerful congressman in the country," speaking of Tom's close connection with Reagan.[32] He had worked his way to the center of political influence and made the most of his time while there.

Reagan called James Watt, secretary of the Interior, and told him to meet Congressman Tom Evans from Delaware and give him the help he needed to pass CBRA. Despite Watt's right-leaning inclination toward the role of government and the environment, he was extremely helpful in ensuring the full backing of the Department of the Interior. Watt's support was crucial in winning support of conservatives and in getting the bill passed.

In a letter from Watt to the Merchant Marine and Fisheries chair Walter Jones (D-N.C.), the secretary provided justification for the proposed bill:

> The barrier islands along the Atlantic and Gulf Coasts are subject to severe erosion by wind, waves and storms. Actions and

programs of the federal government have encouraged development on these islands. When erosion and storm damage occurred, the government has spent substantial amounts of money for disaster relief, projects to stabilize the islands and national flood insurance.

While they are hazardous and expensive for human habitation and development, coastal barriers are excellent habitat for fish and wildlife, and they provide open space and opportunity for public recreation. They create and maintain wetlands and estuaries which nurture vital fish stocks important for commercial and recreational fishing. It is estimated that during some stage in their life history, perhaps as much as 90 percent of all fish caught on the Atlantic and Gulf Coasts are dependent upon the wetlands, which lie behind these geological structures. Coastal barriers and adjacent wetlands provide migration and wintering habitat for migratory waterfowl, shorebirds and raptors, as well as breeding habitat for shore and wading birds. In addition, more than 20 endangered species depend on coastal barrier habitats. For example, sea turtles, all of which are endangered, are totally dependent upon the beaches of coastal barriers as nesting sites.

Millions of people live, work, and vacation near coastal barriers. In fact, over 25 percent of the nation's population lives within 100 miles of the Atlantic and Gulf Coasts. Coastal barriers are central to American life either through direct use and enjoyment or indirectly because they provide habitat to a wide variety of species that disperse to many parts of the nation and benefit large numbers of people.

We believe that legislation along the lines of H.R. 3252 presents an opportunity for substantial savings in direct and indirect federal expenditures, and at the same time recognizes the environmental and recreational values of these unique landforms.

In summary, the benefits of the policy embodied in this legislation are clear. The fish and wildlife and recreation values of these unique landforms can be conserved, and substantial federal expenditures can be saved. While it is difficult to quantify, there can be no question that federal investments have stimulated and facilitated development of storm-prone coastal barriers. The best available estimates during the period beginning with fiscal year 1976 through fiscal year 1980 would indicate that more than a billion dollars was spent by the federal government to aid development on coastal barriers, and that many of these expenditures are not one-time costs. Taxpayers subsidize development, a hurricane sweeps an area, and the government assists, even encourages, rebuilding. The Reconciliation Act and H.R. 3252 chart a sensible course for preventing this cycle from recurring, one that will conserve both tax dollars and natural resources.

The Office of Management and Budget has advised that there is no objection to the presentation of this report from the standpoint of the administration's program.

Step-by-step and congressman-by-congressman, Tom's efforts helped to erode opposition to the bill and gain support from various constituencies. Reagan's gratitude for Tom's unrelenting work on his election campaign proved essential. The president's backing of the bill sealed its fate.

CHAPTER ELEVEN

COASTAL BARRIER RESOURCES ACT FINALIZED

The Congressional Research Service summarized the final bill in this way: "Coastal Barrier Resources Act - Declares the findings and intentions of Congress in regard to the fish, wildlife and other natural resources associated with the coastal barriers along the Atlantic and Gulf Coasts of the United States.

"Establishes the Coastal Barrier Resources System (System) which shall consist of specified undeveloped coastal barriers on the Atlantic and Gulf Coasts.

"Requires that certain coastal barrier maps shall be available for public inspection through the United States Fish and Wildlife Service. Directs the secretary of the Interior to provide copies of such maps to the chief executive officer of: (1) each State and political subdivision in which a System unit is located; and (2) each affected federal agency.

"Authorizes the secretary to make minor modifications to such maps within 180 days. Requires: (1) congressional notification of any such modifications; and (2) review of such maps at least once every five years.

"Limits federal expenditures to specified projects, including energy resource development, military activities, conservation activities, habitat land purchases, channel improvements, road and facility repairs, navigation aids, scientific research projects and emergency assistance.

"Requires the director of the Office of Management and Budget to certify annually to Congress that the federal agencies concerned have complied with the provisions of this Act.

"Requires a System report to Congress within three years. Sets forth such report's content.

"Amends the National Flood Insurance Act of 1968 to prohibit new federal flood insurance as of October 1, 1983, for structures located within the System.

"Authorizes appropriations for F.Y. 1983 through 1985 for the annual reports to Congress."[33]

A snapshot of the comments is highlighted to illustrate the extraordinary effort led and guided by Tom. The first of many accolades begins with John Breaux, chair of the Subcommittee on Fisheries and Wildlife Conservation and the Environment. Once a staunch opponent of the bill, Breaux became one of the driving forces behind its passage. Tom's persistence and influence through gathering co-sponsors, gaining consistent media attention and engaging members of his committee and the entire chamber, forced Breaux not only to change his vote, but support it with the full weight of his position.

Breaux had this to say, in part, in September of 1982 on the House floor:

"Too often, Congress commits its deeds by agent, passing legislation that has substantial effect but, in effect, laundering that effect through bureaucrats and the regulatory process. If we are to deny people federal benefits that are available to other citizens in other areas, we should have the courage to do it directly. By adopting the maps, we have referenced in this legislation, we have accepted our responsibility in this matter.

"Finally, Mr. Speaker, I would like to commend the chief proponent of this legislation in the House, the gentleman from Delaware (Mr. EVANS). He has been very tenacious in pursuing his goal, yet flexible enough to accomplish it. He deserves a great deal of the credit for getting this legislation to where it is today."

Among other remarks about the process, Tom said, "I introduced this bill some 17 months ago, and it is gratifying indeed that we have come this far. In the past 17 months, H.R. 3252 has been very carefully reviewed. Two complete sets of hearings have been held by the Merchant Marine and Fisheries Joint Subcommittees on Fish and Wildlife Conservation and Oceanography. Testimony has been heard from real estate agents, developers, environmental groups, the insurance industry and state, local and federal officials."

Tom went on to say, "Very rarely, if ever, do Democrats and Republicans have an opportunity to vote for a bill that saves lives, saves money and helps protect our environment. And when have you ever seen a bill endorsed by the National Wildlife Federation, the National Taxpayers' Union and the American Red Cross?

"In summary, Mr. Speaker, I want to thank all of those who have worked so hard to bring us to this point, the point toward which we have been working for close to 17 months. I extend my thanks to the National Wildlife Federation and the rest of the Barrier Islands coalition, the distinguished gentleman from Louisiana (Mr. BREAUX), the chairman of our Committee on Merchant Marine and Fisheries, the distinguished gentleman from North Carolina (Mr. JONES), and all of the other members, including those who co-sponsored H.R. 3252, and the subcommittee and full committee staffs, as well as Secretary Watt himself, who, as secretary of the Interior, played a substantial role in this process.

"Very rarely do you see the gentleman from California, Mr. PHILLIP BURTON, get up and praise legislation that has also been praised by the secretary of the Interior, Mr. Watt. And very rarely, if ever, do you see co-sponsors like my friend, the gentleman from Massachusetts (Mr. STUDDS), the gentleman from Kentucky (Mr. SNYDER), the gentleman from Ohio (Mr. SEIBERLING), the gentleman from Oregon (Mr. AUCOIN) and the gentleman from California (Mr. CLAUSEN) co-sponsoring the same piece of legislation. So I would like to thank not only the secretary of the Interior and all the committee staff and members of the committee but all of those who worked so hard to bring us to the point at which we have arrived and consensus where we have a reasonable bill that balances development and environmental interests, that will narrow the federal deficit, that will help save lives, and that will help protect some of the very fertile and vital wetland areas along the Atlantic and Gulf Coasts that are absolutely essential to our nation's economy."

With the completion of opening remarks, the floor opened up to additional comments about the bill and efforts to pass it. The list of speakers and resulting comments were extensive. The feel-good moment was palpable and left a lasting impression on the legislative body about what was possible with an atmosphere of hard work and compromise. There were a few speakers who stood out.

Mr. CLAUSEN. "Mr. Speaker, I wish to extend my congratulations to the gentleman (Mr. EVANS) in the well for his extraordinary leadership in pulling this together, in cooperation with the distinguished leadership of the various committees, this package that I believe will serve not only environmental but also economic objectives.

"I believe the gentleman literally deserves a trophy for perseverance, and I am pleased and proud to be associated with the effort at both committee levels.

"Mr. Speaker, I rise in support of H.R. 3252, the Coastal Barrier Resources Act. This legislation, as it was reported from the Merchant Marine and Fisheries Committee earlier this month, is the result of lengthy negotiations and compromise, and I commend my colleagues for their efforts on this matter."

Mr. SNYDER. "Mr. Speaker, I rise in support of this legislation which would deny federal expenditures and financial assistance on coastal barrier structures along the Atlantic and Gulf Coasts which are not presently developed. Enactment of this legislation will mean that federal expenditures will be reduced by eliminating federal subsidies to storm-prone areas. Also, the measure will help to preserve valuable wetlands which are disappearing at an alarming rate.

"While this proposal has generated a great deal of controversy, I note that many of those originally opposed to the legislation no longer object to its enactment. It is conceded by the former opponents that they will be better off if the bill is enacted.

"The National Association of Realtors, one of the most vocal opponents, is no longer objecting to the committee proposal because it corrects many of the deficiencies in the Interior Department maps which have been drawn up pursuant to the Omnibus Budget Reconciliation Act provisions of 1981. Members who represent districts which would be affected by the legislation have been consulted and, to my knowledge, all disputes concerning their districts have been resolved or otherwise compromised.

"I would like to compliment the gentleman from Delaware (Mr. EVANS) for an excellent job of bringing everyone together to move the bill. Without the gentleman's efforts, I doubt that we would be debating this measure at this time. The chairman of the full committee, Mr. JONES, and the chairman of the Subcommittee on Fisheries and Wildlife Conservation and the Environment, Mr. BREAUX, as well as the subcommittee's ranking minority member, Mr. FORSYTHE, should also be recognized for their hard work and support for this legislation."

Tom's colleague from New Jersey also praised the effort.

Mr. HUGHES. "Finally, I would like to commend the distinguished gentleman from Delaware for his fine work and his personal commitment to this important legislation. I have no doubt that without his personal interest and commitment we would not be considering this bill today."[34]

Gratified and humbled, Tom took in the moment as the praise for the bill and its sponsor unfolded.

The Coastal Barrier Resources Act passed in the House by a remarkable bipartisan vote of 399-

4. In the bill sent to the Senate, there were 129 co-sponsors, including congressmen from 47 states plus Guam, American Samoa and the District of Columbia. Under any circumstances, a nearly unanimous vote on a bill of this magnitude is almost too hard to imagine. Such is the testament to the work Tom, his staff and the supporters invested in the fight.

In the Senate, John Chafee invited Tom to testify prior to the vote. Under the stewardship of the senator from Rhode Island, who was also chair of the Subcommittee on Environmental Pollution, the bill passed easily in the Republican-controlled body. The Coastal Barrier Resources Act was on its way to becoming law.

The only official act left was the president's signature on the bill. Despite widespread support from Congress and constituents and Tom's wishes, the White House chose to keep a low profile on the event — out of the watchful eyes of powerful lobbyists and pro-development donors.

Coastal Barrier Resources Act Finalized

Present at the CBRA bill signing were John Warner, Dick Lugar, Interior Secretary James Watt and Tom.

A year and a half after introducing the bill, on October 18, 1982, Tom witnessed the signing of a historic piece of legislation. It became a lasting marriage of environmental stewardship and fiscal responsibility. Accomplished through a choreographed political ballet and the unrelenting will of a public servant, the Coastal Barrier Resources Act became a symbol of what legislation and the legislative process could be.

Upon signing the bill, President Reagan penned a letter to Tom.

Dear Tom,

Today I was pleased to sign into law the Coastal Barrier Resources Act of 1982 (S.1018).

The enactment of this bill, which you introduced in the House of Representatives, is a classic example of imaginative environmental legislation that is a triumph for natural resource conservation and federal fiscal responsibility. This new law will help to conserve our irreplaceable natural resources of coastal barriers by prohibiting federal assistance for initial or replacement construction and yet does not preclude private development of such areas.

The expeditious passage of the Evans-Chafee bill is a tribute to your leadership abilities and legislative skills.

In recognition of your involvement with the Coastal Barrier Resources Act, please accept this pen which was used to sign the legislation.

Sincerely,

Ronald Reagan

Coastal Barrier Resources Act Finalized

The New York Times would later say that the Coastal Barrier Resources Act became "the most important environmental legislation no one's heard of." Additionally, "The president not only signed it, but did so with a rhetorical flourish, calling it a 'triumph for natural resource conservation and federal fiscal responsibility'."

CBRA initially consisted of 666 miles of shoreline and 452,834 acres of undeveloped, unprotected coastal barriers on the Atlantic Ocean and Gulf of Mexico coasts. While the original CBRA had a tremendous impact on environmental protection, Tom's legislative achievement also laid the groundwork for further conservation. Shortly following its enactment, Congress passed the Great Lakes Coastal Barrier Act, which identified additional System units along the Great Lakes.[36]

The law was amended several times since its passage. According to the Federal Wildlife Service, "The Coastal Barrier Improvement Act (CBIA) of 1990 reauthorized the Coastal Barrier Resources

Act and expanded the Coastal Barrier Resources System by adding new units in Puerto Rico, the U.S. Virgin Islands and the Great Lakes and enlarging some previously designated units along the Atlantic and Gulf Coasts. The CBIA also designated a new category of lands called 'otherwise protected areas' (OPAs).

"The Coastal Barrier Resources Reauthorization Act of 2000 reauthorized the Coastal Barrier Resources Act (CBRA) and directed the U.S. Fish and Wildlife Service to complete a Digital Mapping Pilot Project.

"Other updates to the act were made in 2005 and, most recently, in 2018."[37]

Upon the death of long-time senator and Senate bill sponsor John Chafee in 1999, the system was renamed the John Chafee Resources System.

Coastal Barrier Resources Act Finalized

National Fish and Wildlife map of the Coastal Barrier
Resources System as of March 13, 2019.

CHAPTER TWELVE

THE FALL AND THE RISE AGAIN

D espite his legislative victory, Tom lost his bid for re-election to Tom Carper in November of 1982, one month after the passage of CBRA. It was a blow for him personally and a loss for bipartisanship in Congress.

During his years in Congress, Tom's differences with his wife grew wider and wider and they spent less and less time together. His political success may have been on the rise, but his personal life was on a downward slide. He was a man about town and his gregarious nature led to some serious personal trouble. An affair with Paula Parkinson became public, ultimately ending his political career. But, more importantly, it nearly ended his marriage and his relationship with his three children.

The Fall and the Rise Again

Two weeks after his defeat, a massive fire severely damaged his house. It seemed a fitting metaphor for what was going on in his life. Deep regret followed Tom. All he had worked so hard for lay in ashes at his feet. Coverage in the local paper only served to pour gasoline on his problems — no job, no home and a marriage on the brink.

It was a difficult time for the Evans family, especially for Mary Page and Tom. Although their lives were on different trajectories, hers as an accomplished artist and Tom's as an influential figure in Washington, the struggle forced them to face the truth about their lives and relationship. Since divorce was never on the table, they began the work of gaining back the mutual respect and love for each other that got lost in the pursuit of art shows and political influence.

Although they were cast aside by some, strong friendships and allies remained by their side. Some offered shelter while their house was being rebuilt, and others followed with job opportunities.

Most members of Congress continued their friendship and respect for Tom after he lost his re-election in 1982. One of the members of Congress was Amo Houghton, a former CEO of Corning, Inc. Congressman Houghton, an influential member of the Ways and Means committee, remarked, "He's a darn nice guy, a real friend. He's somebody I can count on."

Tom was offered a position by Washington law firm O'Connor & Hannan as a partner in its legislative affairs office. He lobbied the colleagues he once sat beside on Capitol Hill, but this time Mary Page was by his side, both in Wilmington and Washington. They managed to move forward with their marriage and their life — altered as it was.

In a 1986 *Washington Post* article Mary Page described her experience this way: "No magic moment when everything simply fell into place, no cathartic tears. They just knew that the illusions were gone." Mary Page went on to say, "Art save me from all of this in the end. But the art is what also got me into it . . . I did my own thing all through my marriage. But I paid a price. Listen, I never kid myself. Everything has its price in life and I paid."[38]

Chuck Manatt, chair of the Democratic National Committee, recruited Tom to become a partner in the firm that was later to bear his name — Manatt, Phelps, Rothenberg and Evans. He worked as a lawyer-lobbyist representing countries friendly to the U.S., along with companies he recruited from contacts made throughout his career.

Jamaica was one of those countries. In 1982, Tom was sent to Jamaica by President Reagan via Air Force jet with his wife and daughter to represent the United States at the country's 20th anniversary of independence from the United Kingdom. He attended a parade with the relatively new Prime Minister Edward Seaga, who had ousted his socialist opponent by a landslide two years prior. The pro-capitalist leader was cheered by the U.S. and other Western countries. Tom's presence in 1982 led to retaining the country for his new firm.[39]

He spent the next 20 years continuing his work through lobbying efforts for friends and colleagues, like John Rollins' Environmental Services Company, and other causes, like Jamaica's, that he felt called to support. While the title of "lobbyist" is often met with turned noses, Tom felt called to continue advocating for people, countries, organizations and more throughout his career in Washington. While the environment wasn't the main focus of his lobbying work, he never kept his eyes off the progress he made in Congress.

And though his time as legislator was relatively brief, Tom's work on the environment wouldn't end with a failed election, nor would outside pressure to chip away at environmental protections he worked so hard to enact. The assault against the Coastal Barrier Resources Act and the Alaska Lands Act by those who could benefit financially from land development would continue. Tom brought his will, his gift for connecting people and his voice to fight back in the years to follow for the environment and for other causes he believed in.

PART III

STILL FIGHTING

CHAPTER THIRTEEN

A DIFFERENT KIND OF BATTLE

W hen Tom left office in 1983, he vowed he would not remain silent on salient issues surrounding the environment and climate change. But his advocacy went further. Just as he did in his first month in Congress, he became, and still is, vocal about good government process and politics. If there is a breach of public trust, Tom will call it out. If politicians are led astray by the influence of money or partisanship, he uses his platform to speak truth to power. He continues to be influential in his community and around the country, using speeches, op-eds and good old-fashioned conversation to affect the ever-changing winds of politics.

Digging through his archives reveals mountains of yellow legal pads that line his home office, along with a countless overflow of boxes in his basement. Each is filled with new ideas and rehashed ones he's hoping no one will forget. Throughout the years, he's been asked to speak at gatherings large and small for personal and political events, as well as for charitable, social and, of course, environmental causes. He isn't likely to turn down an invitation.

In his many file drawers live examples of the legacy he leaves and the lives he's touched — speeches at universities, Rotary clubs, golf clubs, lifelong learning academies. The yellow legal pads are the birthing place for most of them.

But he also doesn't wait to be asked to give his opinion. If he sees a news report or reads an article that sparks his enthusiasm or ire, he'll grab a yellow pad and a fresh felt-tipped black marker and pen an op-ed to his local *News Journal,* or set his sights on one of the country's leading newspapers. He'll take aim at political leaders and

CEOs who are either misguided or inept, with hopes of shaping public opinion or exerting political pressure. He's not shy about his disdain for the trajectory of the Republican Party and its leaders, who have ventured far from the GOP of his day. And he still fights hard to maintain the protection of the environment he worked so hard to establish.

Over the years, there have been numerous articles written about him or the legislation he championed. They describe the way he operated to get the job done and the lasting impact of the bills he worked the hardest to pass. There are also awards he received and more-recent projects that bear his fingerprints, even as the years wear on.

This section of the book contains a taste of each of these. The first part focuses on his beloved environment. The second takes a searing look at the changing political landscape. They are a compilation of his words and the words of others who observed or admired him.

Narrowing down the number of articles and speeches and the breadth of the topics covered to include in this book was yeoman's work. His continued dedication to the public interest is notable. What follows is a sampling of how he used his voice to influence this and the next generation of engaged citizens.

CHAPTER FOURTEEN

ATTACK ON THE ENVIRONMENT

As a veteran of the politics surrounding the environment and ubiquitous actors set out to pick apart protections for people, animals and the planet, Tom knew where and when to strike to get noticed. He used his pen and his connections to raise social consciousness about ever-changing climate conditions and development pressures on precious lands. The following examples touch on the work he's done since leaving office, many in the last 20 years.

ALASKA WILDERNESS

Marking the 25th anniversary of the passage of the Alaska Lands Act, the Alaska Conservation Foundation held a weekend celebration in July of 2005. President Jimmy Carter delivered the keynote address on Saturday, and Tom delivered the Sunday keynote to the approximately 500 people gathered. Tom didn't hold back his criticism for George W. Bush's administration or Congress as it related to their collective stance on the environment.

Alaska Conservation Foundation
25th Anniversary of the Alaska Lands Act
Keynote Address
By Tom Evans

Thank you, Bill Meadows, for your introduction and, most importantly, for what you and Becky Rohm and others are doing at the Wilderness Society on behalf of our planet. Thank you, Deborah Williams! Thanks to Congressman Souder for being with us and especially for your work in our national parks. Thanks everyone for being here and for the inspiration you provide. A special thank you to Cindy Shogan, who does such a fine job as executive director of the Alaska Wilderness League.

How long will it be before this administration gets it? How long will it take them to understand that conserving and preserving is a conservative thing to do?

And how long will it take for the Bush Administration and the Republican leadership in Congress to remember that the Republican party has a great heritage in preserving the natural resources we have been so generously given. They should remember that great conservationist and Republican president Teddy Roosevelt and another Republican president, Dwight Eisenhower, set aside the Arctic National Wildlife Refuge's original acreage. And don't forget Richard M Nixon. He did a great deal for Native Alaskans and also established the Environmental Protection Agency. Preserving natural resources, caring about the environment, is not, and should not be, a partisan issue. It belongs to all of us Democrats, Republicans and independents alike!

Perhaps if George W. Bush and Tom DeLay were able to better understand the value of preserving a great treasure like the Arctic National Wildlife Refuge for future generations, they might have second thoughts about drilling for oil there. Perhaps if they were influenced less by large amounts of dollars received from major oil companies like Exxon. Perhaps if they listened less to Dick Cheney, my former colleague and friend who, as head of the energy task force, told us that conservation is only a personal virtue. It does nothing to reduce our dependence on foreign oil. I know where that type of thinking belongs. Maybe Pluto! Perhaps if they read some of Debbie Miller's marvelous children's books, they might change their minds.

Perhaps if we could dispel some myths that the administration and the leadership in Congress seemed to be buying, we might change our minds.

Let's look at those myths.

Myth #1

There's a substantial amount of oil in the coastal plain of ANWR, and if only we could drill there, we would solve our energy problems.

Remember the California energy crisis several years ago? We were told that if only we could drill in the Arctic, we could resolve that energy crisis.

I might also add that there was certainly an implication that one of the benefits from invading Iraq would be lower gasoline prices. That turned out to be false as well, and in the process, we've made this a much more dangerous world.

We already have a glut of oil in the world today. The problem is not supply, but the ability to refine it. And there is just not a substantial amount of oil in ANWR. At best, it will only supply 3 to 4 percent of our energy needs, and it won't come on stream for eight to 10 years. Conoco and British Petroleum, to their credit, are not even going to bid on the leaseholds. Why in the world would we even think about destroying something so very special unnecessarily? For misguided greed?

Why in the world don't we raise fuel economy standards a couple of miles per gallon? Why don't we add just a little more air to our tires? These types of things would be worth more in developing energy independence than all the oil we would ever find in the Arctic.

And, if we have a major push in developing alternative sources of energy, we will create thousands of jobs in science and engineering. I might add that many of those jobs could be right here in this magnificent state of Alaska!

The moguls in the Middle East certainly don't want us to wean ourselves away from our oil consumption. Incredibly, we consume 25 percent of all the energy produced in the world, and we have only 5 percent of the world's population. Think about it. That should tell us something. We must, and we can do better! America should lead the way, and President Bush should reconsider his position on Kyoto.

Myth #2

Drilling in the coastal plain of the Arctic National Wildlife Refuge will not be harmful to this beautiful, fragile plain.

If you believe that, I'll sell you the Brooklyn Bridge or, better yet, one of those bridges from nowhere to nowhere that some politicians would like to build here in Alaska! That's fiscal insanity.

Oil companies can drill on a two-acre footprint, so 1,000 wells would mean only 2,000 acres. That doesn't sound like very much. But that's exactly what they want you to think. Don't you believe it, because it's only the very tip of the iceberg!

The irreparable damage occurs primarily from the logistical support for the drilling. The interconnected pipelines. The roads. The trucks. The helicopters. The planes. The noise they all make. And the airfields. That's what causes the damage. And, in the Arctic, it is irreversible. And this list of dangers doesn't include a major oil spill. We had an anniversary of the Exxon Valdez spill not long ago. That was catastrophic! Why add additional risks?

And, by the way, we have not treated our Native Americans very well in this country. The Gwinch'in tribe, who live in the Refuge, will have their culture and their livelihoods destroyed. And for what? More profit for Exxon.

Well, ladies and gentlemen, should we give up? Should we roll over? Should we accept what some call an inevitable result?

I say we must never, never give up! I know all of you who have done so much to preserve this great American treasure feel the same way!

We must speak for those who have no voice! The mother polar bear with her newborn cub has no voice. The caribou with her newborn calf, the grizzlies, so magnificently described by your wonderful Alaskan poet, Richard Nelson, and 180 species of birds who spend part of their summers on the coastal plain before heading back to places as far away as South America have no voice. We must prevail for them. And most importantly, we must prevail for future generations of Americans. They have no voice either yet.

We have two opportunities to prevent this insanity coming up soon. The budget reconciliation bill will be coming up again in the House and the Senate. That vote taking place calls for drilling in ANWR.

Between now and then, we must act individually and collectively to tell the real truth about the Arctic National Wildlife Refuge. The American people need to send an unmistakable message to Congress and the Bush Administration. It must begin with all of you here who care so much. Come to Washington for a rally on Tuesday, September 20th.

We have two and a half months to organize. And in the meantime, call and write members of Congress. It does make a difference. Let them know that you really care. Call radio talk shows. Write letters to the editors of your newspapers. Share your thoughts with your friends and neighbors. Ask them to do the same. And give what you can afford. And, because of the urgency, I hope you will stretch that a little.

Let me leave you with a thought. *Our destiny as a nation does not lie in plundering the natural resources that we have been so graciously bequeathed, but rather by doing everything possible to protect and preserve these natural*

*treasures for all God's creatures. With your help,
I know we can win! I wish you all Godspeed!*[40]

CLIMATE CHANGE

Fresh off the devastation of Hurricane Sandy's violent blow, Tom made an impassioned plea to lawmakers and citizens to heed the warnings of climate change. Predictions from his time in Congress had manifested in superstorms, rising sea levels and a warmer climate. Fights of the past, despite progress in some areas, continue to plague us. Tom wrote many opinion pieces to address his continued concern and call for action.

"Plan must combine clean energy, conservation."
The News Journal
December 1, 2012
By Tom Evans

Climate change is in part a result of a natural cycle of nature, but also with a substantial assist from mankind. We can't do much about

Mother Nature, but we can do lots of other things that may slow the process. We desperately need an energy plan that not only encourages production of cleaner energy that does not add further to the warming of our planet, but a plan that also encourages conservation. We must reduce the burning of fossil fuels and the spewing of carbon dioxide that add to the greenhouse effect that is making our planet warmer.

We can increase fuel economy standards, and in the process, thousands of engineers and scientists can be given meaningful jobs that help our economy. The automobile companies already have indicated they are up to the challenge. This will not only reduce fossil fuel use, but it will save consumers money by giving them more bang for the buck.

We should and can, through conservation, reduce the amount of energy we use. All of us need to be a part of the effort. Everyone should do their fair share. For example, turning our thermostats up on hot days and down a touch on cold days will make a difference. Wearing a little extra clothing in winter and less in summer is not too difficult a task.

Another very important element in any credible energy plan is the development of alternative sources of energy: wind, solar, nuclear and natural gas. We have a great deal of natural gas right here in the United States, and it will, in time, help us to reduce the use of coal and oil substantially. In the process, the United States will move away from our dependence on foreign oil from unstable regions in the world. This also makes good sense from the standpoint of national security.

There's a lot riding on our ability to implement an energy plan that addresses the problems we continue to face. In the meantime, the melting of Arctic ice and glaciers that provide water for half of our planet continues, and that creates enormous problems, especially in the undeveloped areas of the world. We must reduce the burning of fossil fuels, and America must lead the way.

We recently have seen an increase in the intensity of storms that cause such bad beach erosion and create storm surges that destroy properties and place so many lives at risk. Sandy's devastation should remain forever etched in our minds. Mankind's significant contribution to climate change may be doubted by a few, but it is for real, and we have a profound responsibility to do everything possible to slow the process.

In the meantime, we also need to adapt to the dangers created by increasingly vicious storms. We need to stop encouraging development through government subsidies in storm-prone vulnerable areas. We cannot prevent development, but we should and can say to those developing, "Do it on your own nickel and not the American taxpayers'."

Fortunately, there is an existing law, The Coastal Barrier Resources Act, that prevents subsidies, including Federal Flood Insurance on undeveloped barrier lands along the Atlantic and

Gulf Coasts. It initially was opposed by many well-funded special interests, but the common-sense approach Congress took in passing the Coastal Barrier Resources Act was not only a tribute to common sense but a fine example of Democrats and Republicans working together to achieve success.[41]

"The Sea's Power and Foolish Policies"
The News Journal
July 3, 2015
By Tom Evans

If Mother Nature cooperates, the Fourth of July weekend is a perfect time to be at the Delaware beaches. Just watching the waves gives an onlooker a small hint of the power of the ocean. Again, if Mother Nature cooperates, the waves will be small and Delawareans and visitors, young and old, can enjoy the sand and the surf.

However, Mother Nature does not always cooperate. As we know from recent history, powerful storms can come churning up the coastline, sucking away sand from the beaches and crashing waves on structures close to the water.

In 2011, Hurricane Irene banged into the East Coast. Hurricane Sandy followed in 2012, at first threatening a direct hit on Delaware, then swerving and smashing into New Jersey and New York. Irene cost $15.8 billion, while Sandy cost $128 billion. This review is not to frighten beachgoers, nor is it to argue that we should take climate change seriously, although that would be a good idea.

No, the review is to remind us how close we are to that powerful sea. Swimmers and splashers are not the problem. The buildings and communities built so close to the beach are. Rebuilding them was what was so expensive about Irene and Sandy. That money comes from taxpayers who probably never even stayed in one of those beachfront properties.

Guess what. They will be paying for the next cleanup as well.

The paradox is that taxpayers are subsidizing people to live the good life near a rising sea. Forget the environmental arguments against this. Just consider the waste of tax money.

The support comes in the form of federally subsidized flood insurance, as well as federal rebuilding efforts and federal funding for roads, sewer lines and other infrastructure.

Is it good for local business? Certainly. But only a limited few benefit from it. There are other, more reasonable ways of enjoying the beaches.

First, do not build so close to the sea. Second, make those who build in those areas pay their own way. Slowly reduce the flood insurance subsidies, develop a policy of not rebuilding again and again.

In 1982, Congress passed the Coastal Barrier Resources Act of 1982. It saved millions of acres of shoreline from development simply by withholding those federal subsidies.

These preserved areas are important because they are the first line of defense against the storms.

Those wetlands and dunes absorb the power of the major storms. Development destroys these barriers. Just look at what happened to the New Orleans region with Hurricane Katrina. Development over decades destroyed the natural defenses.

If you are at the beach, take a moment to consider the power of the sea. Then ask why we are being so foolish.[42]

Well into his 80s, Tom continues to be a strong voice for the environment and for good environmental policy, as evidenced by his 2018 *New York Times* editorial.

"Scott Pruitt, Protecting his own environment"
The New York Times
April 25, 2018
By Tom Evans

You could search the world over and never find a more inappropriate person to head the

Environmental Protection Agency than Scott Pruitt. Although President Trump, who appointed Mr. Pruitt, is not part of the great legacy of Republican presidents who cared about the environment, there is a fine record for many of them.

It started with Teddy Roosevelt, who set aside millions of acres of public land and established a number of national parks. Years later, Dwight Eisenhower set aside as wilderness several million acres in the Arctic National Wildlife Refuge in Alaska. Then Richard Nixon established the Environmental Protection Agency and, unlike Mr. Trump, appointed outstanding leaders there. Ronald Reagan signed into law the Coastal Barrier Resources Act, which has saved over a million acres of storm-prone, vulnerable land.

Sadly, today's Republican leadership does not appreciate the value of preserving wildlife and natural resources.[43]

BRINY BREEZES

In Palm Beach County, Florida, sits the small coastal town of Briny Breezes. Located on a barrier island on Florida's east coast, it also includes Tom's winter home in nearby Delray Beach. The community is primarily made up of mobile homes and sits at or slightly below sea level. While the homes are modest, the land is valuable.

In 2007, residents voted to sell the rights to the property and the entire town of Briny Breezes to real estate development company Ocean Land Investments for $510 million. The developer planned to completely revamp the town to include multiple high-rise buildings up to 20 stories tall, including 900 condominium units, a 349-room luxury hotel, 300 timeshare units, restaurants, shopping and an expanded yacht marina.

While the proposal was a windfall for residents of Briny Breezes, it caught the immediate ire of nearby residents, adjacent town governments and environmentalists. The reasons were varied, but the potential impact of the massive influx of people to the area mobilized a wide-ranging constituency to oppose the plan.

Within a month of the plan being made public, Tom helped found a new group, Florida Coalition for Preservation, and became its first chairman. Like his efforts during the CBRA negotiations, he worked tirelessly with others to form a broad coalition to ensure intense media exposure and public pressure. Press releases, letters to the editor and public meetings were the catalyst of the movement that helped gather momentum for a nearly overwhelming email and letter-writing campaign to state and local officials. Schools and universities, small business owners and environmentalists, churches and synagogues, banded together in a show of immense force.

Objections to the proposal echoed the arguments made for enacting the Coastal Barrier Resources Act 25 years earlier. Among the objections were logistical problems of increased traffic, water demand and sewage production. Development endangered the sea turtle population and could have led to reef destruction and loss of habitat for native creatures. And lastly, overtaxing the fragile barrier island would decrease its ability to serve as protection from storms and make it more difficult to evacuate people in the event of increasingly powerful storms. Of course, nearby residents were also protecting their beloved community.

Tom hired Jane West, an environmental lawyer, to work with the Coalition to strengthen their legal objectives. She made the battle her top priority. At a packed event in Tallahassee that left much of the opposition on the wrong side of the door, Jane lobbied Gov. Charlie Crist in front of TV cameras and other media. The governor took notice of the coalition's objections.

The group also raised a substantial amount of money. Tom's friends Stretch Gardiner, head of Morgan Stanley, his wife Liz and Lynda Stokes invited 125 people to the Gardiner's winter home in Florida for a reception to support the effort. The guest list included many members of the Gulf Stream Golf Club.

A week prior at a small dinner party, Tom's friend, Lee Brown, former U.S. Ambassador to Austria, had arranged for him to sit next to Lee's mother, the matriarch of the Brown family that owns Brown Forman, distillers of spirits and wines, including Jack Daniels.

After Tom spoke at the party at the Gardiner's, Mrs. Brown rose from the only chair in the room and made an impassioned plea to support Tom and his good work. She was the first to hand him a check. Others soon followed, stuffing Tom's pockets as he walked through the room. Although contributions were limited to $10,000 per person, the event and subsequent donations over the next few weeks netted an impressive $500,000 for the cause.

The coalition issued its first press release soon after its formation in the spring of 2007. In his role as chairman, Tom wrote, "This coalition supports reasonable and responsible development that respects the area's character and environment." The release included remarks from former secretary of the Florida Department of Community Affairs Thaddeus Cohen, Ed Tichenor of Palm Beach County Reef Rescue, Max Mayfield, former director of the National Hurricane Center, Ocean Ridge Mayor Ken Kaleel and Palm Beach County Commissioner Mary McCarty. The impressive list of coalition members gathered and engaged in a matter of weeks is a testament to Tom's experience as an organizer and coalition builder.[44]

The opposition was organized, well-funded and thoughtful in its approach. Swift and bold action by the coalition, led by Tom, resulted in the developer pulling the deal. Even after the crisis was averted, the Florida Coalition for Preservation remained intact, and still operates to protect the local area from the dangers of overzealous development.

LECTURES AT COLLEGES AND UNIVERSITIES

For many years, Tom used his experience and expertise to teach the next generation of citizens. Although he spoke about good government, foreign policy and politics, he also used his podium to inspire students in environmental stewardship. The following excerpt is from one of his lectures.

"Energy, Conservation and the Environment"
Florida Atlantic University
April 14, 2005
By Tom Evans

The older I get, the more I'm concerned about the future. And nowhere is the need for a longer-term view more apparent than in our environment. The air we breathe, the water we drink, the food we eat. It's critical. It should not be political.

Why do some (many of the Republicans in the House and Senate), and certainly President Bush and Vice President Cheney, think that we must choose between economic prosperity and environmental protection? Why don't they understand that jobs and good environmental policies are not competing values? Why do they think that those who care about the environment don't care about jobs? Why do we treat our planet as if it's a business that's being liquidated? Why do a number of Republicans and others that I know refer to environmentalists as 'enviros' in a most disparaging manner? Why did Dick Cheney, who headed the Energy Task Force a few years ago, state that conservation may be a personal virtue, but it does nothing to reduce our dependency on foreign oil?

Is it just ignorance or stupidity? Probably not. Is it a lack of understanding or a lack of vision or a lack of interest in the future? Probably, but, in my view, it might be a result of huge contributions from those that care much more about the bottom line today than they do about the future.

Attack on the Environment

As we have previously discussed, the administration and others are doing everything they can to create a sense of crisis surrounding Social Security. It's the same administration that created a crisis regarding the imminent threat of weapons of mass destruction held by Saddam Hussein in Iraq. Making mistakes in Social Security or tax policy, or even foreign policy, creates problems, but not irreversible ones. But in the environmental field, much of what is being done we cannot correct, or at least not in our lifetimes. That's where the real crisis lies, and it is for real. This planet is under stress, and we must address the problems with the full knowledge that the political atmosphere in which we live makes it difficult, but not impossible.

Let me give you an idea or two of what we are up against in battling the administration of George W. Bush and Richard Cheney, combined with the Republican leaders in the House and Senate. The environment is under siege, and they hold a lot of the cards.

First and foremost, and especially for the future, President Bush's model for a Supreme Court justice is Clarence Thomas. He has said that Congress should not have any jurisdiction over establishing environmental standards. Looking ahead, that is a problem of crisis proportions. The chairman of the Senate Environment and Public Works Committee, James Inhofe of Oklahoma, has said that global warming is, in his own words, 'a hoax.' He, and many, believe that climate change is a myth, and sea levels aren't rising. But that flies in the face of science. I don't know a reputable or well-known scientist who does not hold the view that CO_2 (carbon dioxide) is a major contributing factor in creating a greenhouse effect in the earth's atmosphere that is warming this planet. James Watt, who was Interior secretary in the '80s, said that protecting natural resources was unimportant in light of the imminent return of Jesus Christ. Many in the so-called Christian Right believe this as well, and they are sincere, polite and serious. They believe the Messiah will return for the rapture and that environmental destruction is not only to be disregarded, but some actually feel that it should be hastened as a sign of the coming of the apocalypse. Forty-five senators and 186 House members earned 80-100 percent approval ratings from the top three Christian Right advocacy groups.

Zell Miller, a mean-spirited, divisive Democratic senator from Georgia who gave the keynote address at the Republican Convention last summer, received a 100 percent rating. And, ladies and gentlemen, not one single time has President Bush even mentioned the word 'environment' or 'conservation' in his State of the Union address (at least not in the last two). By the way, they were not mentioned at the Republican National Convention in New York. That's a fairly clear indication of where the administration stands on conservation and the environment.

Well, what can be done? Is it hopeless? I think not. Let me review with you some very specific facts and problems related to energy, conservation and the environment. I especially want to share with you several initiatives with which I am intimately involved.

First, we produce 5 percent of all the energy produced in the world, and we use 25 percent of all the energy that is used in the world. Our total oil and gas reserves in the United States are about 5 percent of the total in the world. That leads us to only one conclusion. We must develop alternative sources of energy – hydroelectric, wind, solar, nuclear. (Some of my colleagues in the environmental field disagree with me about nuclear, but it is the cleanest form of energy.) And we need conservation. We need to increase fuel economy standards, despite Mr. Cheney's statement about conservation being only a personal virtue.

Although the facts and reason dictate otherwise, the administration seems obsessed with drilling in the Arctic National Wildlife Refuge. Over two decades ago, the Alaska National Interest Lands Conservation Act passed the House and Senate. Most of the action on that bill was in the

House, and it passed, supported by a true bipartisan coalition of Democrats and Republicans. That law, and especially the protection it afforded the fragile coastal plain of the Arctic National Wildlife Refuge, is now being threatened by a Republican administration and a Republican-led Congress.

As a former Republican Congressman deeply involved in the passage of the Alaska Lands Act almost 25 years ago, I like to remind my Congressional colleagues that the Republican Party has a rich history of preserving the natural resources we have been so generously bequeathed. Teddy Roosevelt, Dwight Eisenhower, Richard Nixon all left legacies we can be proud of.

Apparently, the President and the Republican leadership in Congress fail to recognize that preservation is a conservative thing to do. The American people deserve the facts, and they, in turn, need to communicate with members of Congress that they should not make decisions based on myths.

Let me share with you some information about another initiative I've been working on for the last year. The Interior Appropriations bill calls for the American taxpayer to fund additional logging roads in the Tongas Forrest in Alaska. These funds end up in the pockets of large timber companies. We should clearly cut this type of corporate welfare that encourages more clear-cutting of timber. It is nonsensical. I believe we will be successful in eliminating this totally misguided move by the administration, and most importantly, it will be done by a coalition of Democrats and Republicans.

Let me give you some more facts that support my premise that this administration and this Congress must wake up, and they will only do so if people demonstrate that they care.

During the last four years, there has been a 50 percent reduction in enforcement actions against polluters, a 34 percent decline in criminal penalties and a 50 percent decline in civil penalties for environmental crimes. And ladies and gentlemen, I mentioned earlier that the president never mentioned the environment or conservation in any of his State of the Union addresses or at the Republican National Convention. Let me add that he did not mention global warming, clean air, clean water or pollution one time in any of his State of the Union addresses or at the Republican National Convention!

And that leads us to the Kyoto Accord. We use 25 percent of all the energy consumed in the world. We should work with others to reduce CO_2 emissions that cause global warming for many reasons, but especially since global warming affects this entire planet. The administration has dragged its feet and continues to say that the science is not clear. That's just not true. It is true that we would have to do more than other nations, but remember we are the biggest users of energy by far, and we are the strongest! I know the Kyoto Accords are not perfect, but we shouldn't walk away from them like a spoiled child who couldn't get everything he or she wanted. We should stay involved and play a leadership role. We are the only industrialized nation in the world that is not a part of Kyoto, and that is sad. Among other things, it certainly does not help us in our relations with other countries. And, my friends, we need to have, if not their friendship, at least their respect, and we'll address that issue in our lecture on April 20 (two weeks from today) on foreign policy and national security.

We're just not doing a very good job in education. For example, how many of us, and that includes politicians who represent us, know much about the value of wetlands? They have been destroyed at a rapid clip, and we have not done a very good job of connecting the dots between wetlands and pollution control and flood control. Wetlands are like a sponge; they filter out pollution and they do a lot to prevent flooding. And without them, we don't have oystering and clamming and sport fishing or commercial fishing. They are spawning grounds for fish and shellfish, and clearly, they are habitat areas for all kinds of wildlife. They are an extremely valuable resource and critically important to our economy. We need to start educating our citizens at a very early age.

Some of this is happening, but, because it has not always been a focus early on, the media in this country needs to help connect those dots and hold politicians accountable for their actions. A lot is riding on it.

Let me just cover a few more areas in which you may have an interest.

Clean air: we need to connect the dots here. Utilities that produce nitrogen oxide and sulfur dioxide, NOX and SOX it's called, do great damage to people's health. Utilities are also big contributors to global warming through carbon dioxide emissions. The administration tried unsuccessfully to rewrite the Clean Air Act and give utilities more time to comply with Clean Air Act standards. The law said that if you expanded your capacity significantly, you would have to use state-of-the-art emission controls. By the way, these emissions cause big problems with people who have asthma and other respiratory diseases that are greatly exacerbated by the soot and smog created by polluters. Incidentally, we should all bear in mind that there are costs to upgrade facilities, but there is a heavy price to pay in costs of healthcare if they are not upgraded. More people are hospitalized and lose time from work, and this clearly affects productivity. It's one of those hidden costs of pollution.

Since the bill the administration was pushing took away states' rights to sue other states, it failed in committee. All the Democrats, plus Lincoln Chafee on the Republican side, voted against it.

In one of the few environmental initiatives of this administration, the EPA issued a rule last month that implemented some controls over emissions of harmful pollutants. Unfortunately, it doesn't go into effect until the year 2015. But it's some progress. The rule also tries to cut the costs of cutting pollution by allowing power plants to buy and sell emission credits. As a result, the cost per month for customers in the dirtiest states will be less on average than $1 per month, probably 60-70 cents. One of the most deadly pollutants is mercury that finds its way into rivers, bays and lakes, and yes, the ocean as well. The fish absorb it, and people eat fish. That's just a part of the cycle, and I think that, as far as mercury is concerned, because of its very nature, there should be no emission credits.

There are a number of lawsuits at the moment, including one in the U.S. Court of Appeals for the District of Columbia. The administration has reversed a Clinton administration policy that permitted the EPA to regulate carbon dioxide emissions from motor vehicles. The administration's position is that the science is unclear about whether CO_2 (carbon dioxide) contributes to global warming. This particular lawsuit turns on whether Section 202 of the Clean Air Act applies. It states, "the EPA Administrator shall regulate any air pollutant from any new vehicles that may reasonably be anticipated to endanger public health or welfare."

The number of blocked federal judges skyrocketed during the Clinton administration as partisanship increased. I bring this up to demonstrate the importance of appointments to the various federal courts. They are critical. Let's look quickly at the Clean Water Act, and here, I believe, the government has done a reasonable job of regulation from the standpoint of utilities and industrial plants. Where they have not done a good job is in what they call non-point source situations. Translated, that means run-off from agriculture, municipalities and others where the source of the pollution is a little more difficult to determine.

By the way, the oceans take up two thirds of the earth's surface, and there are limits to what they can assimilate. Ocean dumping, once thought to be the answer to the world's sludge and trash problem, highlights shortsightedness and expedience over prudent long-range planning.

Let's turn, for a moment, to contaminated industrial sites. They are not contained, and they leak. The Superfund program has slowed to a crawl. The financial resources in the Superfund Trust Fund have plummeted, starved by the expiration of a "polluter pays" tax on chemicals and oil products. The administration is looking for general tax revenues to finance clean-up on a pay-as-you-go basis. No longer do they want to use the "polluter pays" principle. You don't have to be a rocket scientist to figure that out!

We need to be more creative in recycling, for example, and think of ways in which we might jump start the revitalization of our older communities by investing more in the clean-up of former manufacturing sites. Investing in our environment can go hand in hand with economic growth. And there should be planning for growth that is tied to the availability of water, and we must engage in long-range transportation planning. We can assist local and state governments as they tackle the problem of sprawl. That's in part what the Coastal Barrier Resources Act was all about.[45]

BATTLE FOR THE BARRIERS FILM

In 2015, Tom and his wife Mary Page sat with anticipation at the Delaware Theatre Company awaiting the premier of a new documentary, *Battle for the Barriers*. Produced by fellow Wilmingtonian Sharon Baker, the 32-minute film features the continued battle to protect fragile barrier lands against nature and development. Sharon sought to highlight the Coastal Barrier Resources Act and the work of the many environmental and research groups working to save the land for the future.

Many years back, Sharon met Tom in her role as a reporter with local radio station, WILM. Tom and Mary Page hosted a Christmas party in their home for local reporters to stop in and share a little holiday cheer. The charm and hospitality of the hosts continued long after the party ended. Sharon was often invited to dinners over the years, and she, in turn, invited their daughter Page to intern with her video production company, Teleduction.

One evening over dinner, Tom and Sharon talked about the environment and the shore, which they both frequented. And, as Tom loves to do, he shared the story of how CBRA came to be. As a filmmaker, Sharon was captivated and intrigued by the idea of bringing this story to life. There was no one more ready and equipped to make that happen than Tom.

With its 501c3 status, Teleduction raised money to cover costs of filming and production. While Tom used his extensive contacts and his own money to raise funds, he also connected Sharon with current experts in the field. She described Tom as "instrumental to the project and a great interview." He didn't try to influence the direction of the film, and he put her in touch with the right people to make the project work. Once the idea caught fire, they energized each other to its completion.

One of those connections was Manley Fuller, president of the Florida Wildlife Federation (FWF). Tom served on the board with him at the

FWF for years. Sharon described Manley as a "detective" with so much information.

"His enthusiasm and energy are remarkable," Sharon says of Tom. Of his work on CBRA, "He was ahead of his time."

With a shared vision for the film, they offer it free of charge to educational and community groups. They still hope for wider distribution and more awareness of the protection provided by CBRA, and the threats to its existence. As of this printing, the documentary is available on Vimeo.com and Amazon Prime Video.

NATIONAL WILDLIFE FEDERATION

In December of 2015, Tom received a letter from the National Wildlife Federation president and CEO, Collin O'Mara. Nominated by longtime colleague Manley Fuller, the letter informed Tom that he had earned a special award.

Here is the letter Tom received.

Dear Congressman,

On behalf of the National Wildlife Federation, I am pleased to inform you that our board of directors has voted to honor you with a special award for your leadership on conservation.

Your longtime dedication to help protect and maintain America's natural resources and landscapes are an inspiration and exemplify the National Wildlife Federation's goals of safeguarding wildlife and connecting people to nature. In particular, we want to recognize your leadership in helping enact two landmark conservation laws, the Coastal Barrier Resources Act and the Alaska National Interest Lands Conservation Act.

Unlike many other elected officials, you also continued to champion these and other conservation causes after you left Congress and right up to the present. You have remained a forceful and effective advocate for protecting our barrier islands, for flood insurance reform, for protection of the Arctic National Wildlife Refuge and other key issues. Your partnership and engagement with the Florida Wildlife Federation over the past seven years led to a number of successful initiatives and programs.

You have truly been an inspiration and we would be thrilled if you would allow us to honor you at our 2016 National Wildlife Federation annual meeting.

With Tom and Mary Page are Landon Hilliard III, Manley Fuller, Collin O'Mara and other members of the NWF presenting the award.

Tom was deeply honored to receive this award. Although he is no longer active in the Florida Wildlife Federation, he continues to support the state and national organizations.

More recently, environmental groups from up and down the Eastern seaboard and led by the National Wildlife Federation collaborated on a letter to David Bernhardt, secretary of the Interior, pleading for reversal of a decision to allow sand mining within the Coastal Barrier Resources System. While CBRA stands as the ideal of what good environmental policy can be, attacks continue to breech its impact.

Dear Secretary Bernhardt,

On behalf of our more than six million members and supporters, the National Wildlife Federation, along with our affiliate partners from California, Connecticut, Delaware, Florida, Georgia, Hawaii, Maryland, Massachusetts, New Hampshire,

New Jersey, New York, North Carolina, Pennsylvania, Puerto Rico, Virginia and the Virgin Islands, urges you to reverse the recent decision that would allow federally funded sand mining within the Coastal Barrier Resources System (CBRS) for use in non-CBRS areas. This decision is contradictory to the longstanding interpretation and intent of the Coastal Barrier Resources Act (CBRA), which was designed to safeguard ecologically rich, sensitive coastal areas from federally-funded development, protecting both people and wildlife. For decades, CBRA's free-market approach to environmental protection has saved taxpayer dollars, promoted public safety and protected our coastal environment. We ask that you withdraw the new interpretation of the law, and reinstate the interpretation used by this and previous administrations for the last twenty-five years, which prohibits federal expenditures to mine sand within CBRS areas for use in other areas outside the system.

The National Wildlife Federation is America's largest and oldest conservation organization, collaborating with 52 state and territorial affiliates to serve as a voice for wildlife and for millions of hunters, anglers, and outdoor enthusiasts. Our organizations have long worked to protect and restore our nation's coasts, barrier islands, wetlands, and floodplains – areas that provide some of the most vital fish and wildlife habitat. These same areas also help protect coastal communities by serving as buffers against storm surge, wave action, and floods.

The CBRA program encourages the protection of 3.5 million acres of ecologically valuable coastal floodplains by withholding federal taxpayer funding and subsidies that promote risky development in these vulnerable areas, safeguarding important habitat for fish and wildlife. This important tool helps protect coastal communities, economies, and fish and wildlife – and has saved Americans billions of dollars in avoided federal expenditures since it was passed in 1982. The free-market approach to coastal conservation that CBRA promotes has generated strong bipartisan support for the program since its creation, most recently demonstrated by Congress' nearly unanimous passage of legislation updating CBRS maps and adding more than 18,000 acres to the System.

This policy shift allowing federal funds to be used for sand mining within the CBRS can be expected to significantly increase the practice, resulting in devastating impacts on fish and wildlife species and habitat, including nesting shorebirds, migratory birds, sea turtles, fisheries, water quality and benefit communities, subsequently impacting local commercial and recreational fishing and tourism economies. In addition to negative impacts to fish and wildlife, sand mining can also cause increased erosion of adjacent shorelines, reducing coastal resilience.

As noted in the report that accompanied Senate passage of the CBRA, "This legislation recognizes that coastal barriers should be conserved in their natural state for two reasons. First . . . . these areas provide essential habitat for fish and wildlife. Secondly, it is evident that federal tax dollars encourage development . . . and then perpetuate that development . . . Federal expenditures which subsidize and thereby encourage development in these dynamic areas constitute an unwise investment ... By aiding development of coastal barriers, the federal government is diminishing the productivity of estuaries and wetlands in terms of fish and wildlife resources; increasing risks to life and property; and, reducing the capacity of such areas to protect the mainland from storms."

Allowing the expenditure of federal dollars for sand mining within CBRS units for nourishment activities elsewhere would run contrary to the objectives of the CBRA. This activity does not benefit or support the purposes for which CBRS units were created, nor is it supported by an accompanying assessment of possible economic or ecological impacts or an official opportunity for public review or comment. The lack of public engagement from the Department of Interior around a decision with such far-reaching ramifications is deeply troubling.

CBRS units were established to safeguard taxpayer dollars, promote public safety by discouraging risky new coastal development, and support healthy coastal wildlife and habitats. Allowing federally funded sand mining within the CBRS is contrary to the letter and spirit of the CBRA and would harm some of the most valuable remaining fish and wildlife habitat along our coasts. Our organizations strongly urge you to withdraw this new opinion and reinstate the prior interpretation of the CBRA that is consistent with the purposes of the law.

Sincerely,

Connecticut Forest & Park Association
Conservation Council for Hawai'i
Delaware Nature Society
Environmental Advocates of New York
Environmental League of Massachusetts
Florida Wildlife Federation
Georgia Wildlife Federation
National Aquarium
National Wildlife Federation
New Hampshire Audubon
New Jersey Audubon
North Carolina Wildlife Federation
Penn Future Planning and Conservation League
Sociedad Ornitológica Puertorriqueña, Inc.
Virginia Conservation Network
Virgin Islands Conservation Society

CHAPTER FIFTEEN

GOOD GOVERNMENT

G ood government practices and the environment are not, as Tom has repeatedly emphasized, mutually exclusive. Tom meets the changing politics, and his party, head on, taking aim at cabinet-level bureaucrats and individual congressmen on Capitol Hill on many topics, above and beyond the environmental issues so dear to him. And he saves his most fervent criticism for party leaders, including the president.

While he is perhaps now more of a Democrat at heart, he keeps the R attached to his name to try to influence the party from within. As the party of Lincoln and Reagan strays further from its roots, Tom is here to remind its members of what's at stake when you sell out to the highest bidder and leave the people and planet behind.

Here's some of his insight on the matter, using his own words from speeches and op-eds.

"Count Them All Again"
***Washington Post* Editorial**
November 18, 2000
By Tom Evans

Nothing should have a higher priority than the integrity of our political process. Not Vice President Al Gore, or Gov. George W. Bush, or the Republican Party or the Democratic Party. Florida Secretary of State Katherine Harris will have irretrievably darkened the cloud that already hangs over the presidential election if her decision on Wednesday to ignore hand-counted revised tallies is permitted to stand.

Harris has declared her intention to certify the statewide results after overseas absentee ballots have been counted, the expectation being that those votes will add to Bush's current 300 vote lead. Yesterday, a Florida Circuit Judge refused to order her to accept results of manual vote recounts that could give the lead to Al Gore.

Throughout the campaign, Bush promised that he was the kind of guy who was a uniter and not a divider. He promised to bring people together, not push them farther apart. His representatives now need to cool their rhetoric; and if they cannot, they need to be placed in a political deep freeze.

Similarly, Al Gore should rigidly enforce his good and well-expressed intentions. Bush does not want hand recounts limited only to Broward and Palm Beach counties, ostensibly because they could be subject to fraud. It is also true that the results would almost certainly tilt in Al Gore's favor. I believe that is precisely why Secretary Harris took the position she did.

But hand counts do not necessarily have to be inaccurate or prone to fraud. It all depends on the manner in which they are conducted. There have already been recounts in several Florida counties, six of which had majorities for George W. Bush. In addition, we should bear in mind that for at least the first 150 years of our nation's history, hand counts were the only way to count votes and they were accepted as fair and legitimate.

Getting it right is clearly more important than meeting an arbitrary deadline with flawed and questionable results. George W. Bush has understandably rejected a hand recount limited only to Broward and Palm Beach counties because of their overwhelmingly Democratic registration.

Therefore, it seems to me that the only fair course would be to conduct a time-limited hand recount in all 67 of Florida's counties, using clear and consistent criteria for these recounts. Surely, both Gov. Bush and Vice President Gore should agree to such a resolution.

Yes, there needs to be finality for this unbelievable situation (and Gore has finally committed to a recount ending in one week). But of utterly more importance is to get it right. The votes need to be counted accurately, fairly and honestly in Florida. Unless that happens, the next presidency will be a flawed one indeed, and our country and this world could suffer irreparable harm.

America needs to come together, and with razor-thin margins in both the House and Senate, we do, in fact, need someone who can unite and not divide. That person could be a President Bush or a President Gore. However, it will be neither one unless the American people accept the results in Florida as honestly representing the will of the voters in the Sunshine State.[46]

"Is Our Government Working for You?"
Forum at Florida Atlantic University
December 9, 2006
By Tom Evans

Welcome to this forum today, and thank you for caring about what's happening in the world and in our country. We face some critical challenges, and I've always respected those who search for knowledge and truth and who believe that this search is a lifelong journey.

Today, we will be addressing a number of critical issues — some of them are quite controversial. I hope we will be guided by the words of Thomas Jefferson. He said, "Here we are not afraid to follow truth wherever it may lead, so long as reason is free to combat it!" That's the spirit we need to foster not just here today, but throughout the country and indeed the world. We must encourage people everywhere to listen and to respect others.

We are privileged and honored today to have with us three outstanding Americans.

The Honorable Ann Brown, a former chairman of the Consumer Products Safety Commission, nominated by President Bill Clinton. Chairman Brown has been an outstanding advocate for consumers in America, and especially for the safety of our children.

Never timid about speaking out, she served in the leadership of the Consumer Federation of America and is the recipient of many top national honors. Chairman Brown spent most of her undergraduate years at Smith College, and graduated from George Washington University.

Mr. Julian Gingold has advised many presidents, especially on trade, but also on our economy and politics. Julian has an encyclopedic knowledge of political history. That knowledge, combined with his judgement, has made him a sought-after advisor for many Republicans running for the presidency, for Congress, for governor and other races. Occasionally, he will even give advice to Democrats. He has served on a number of presidential commissions.

Julian Gingold graduated from the Wharton School at the University of Pennsylvania. He is a senior vice president of UBS — Union Bank of Switzerland.

Michael Dukakis is the longest-serving governor in the history of Massachusetts — 12 years, but not consecutive, starting in 1974-1978, again from 1982-1986 and 1986-1990. He has an outstanding record, and among his many accomplishments he attracted a number of high-tech companies to Massachusetts. He was the Democratic standard bearer for president in 1988. Before the negative advertising began against him, he was just under 20 points ahead of George Herbert Walker Bush, who became president.

Gov. Dukakis shares his knowledge and experience with all ages. He is a professor at UCLA, Northeastern University and NYU. Michael Dukakis is a graduate of Swarthmore College and the Harvard Law School, and as many of you know, taught right here at FAU for four years.

It's an honor to have you and all these very fine Americans here with us today.

Now, let me lead off this forum, where we will be discussing whether or not our government is working for you. That depends to a certain degree on who "you" is!

Our Constitution set up three separate but equal branches of government. The founding fathers were especially concerned about giving too much power to the executive branch of government. Over the last 200-plus years, our constitutional democracy has been the foundation for a country that has given our citizens great freedom and opportunity.

We have been respected by free nations around the globe, not just for our military might or the strength of our economy, but for our values. That respect has been eroded but certainly not irreversibly.

The freedom we have always enjoyed has tested succeeding generations of Americans again and again. We have most always met that test in preserving the principles set forth in our Constitution but — in the final analysis — it depends on an enlightened electorate and the people they select to lead.

Let me share with you a message from one of those leaders in a lame-duck session of the U.S.

House of Representatives in December of 1977. Hubert Humphrey rose to speak after being introduced by Mo Udall. The chamber was packed, and he was thin, suffering from cancer with less than six weeks to live. He walked up to the podium just above the House floor. Smiling and in a very clear voice he said, "You know, my friends, I've spent close to a lifetime trying to get to this podium and I've finally made it!"

It was a poignant moment and everyone in the chamber rose to their feet. There was genuine affection in the loud and sustained ovation. Vice President Humphrey's message was to make our democracy work.

He had a message for Democrats and Republicans. To the Republicans, he reminded us that under our system, the majority prevails. However, his real message was to the Democrats who held overwhelming majorities in both houses of Congress. To them he said, "If you trample on the rights of the minority, if you don't treat them with respect and permit their participation, you are not only harming this body, you are damaging our country greatly!"

But, ladies and gentlemen, the Republican leadership in the House and the leadership at the White House today have not heeded the words of Hubert Humphrey. And, as far as the White House is concerned, they have not communicated very well with Democrats or Republicans.

Look at where our country is at this point in our history.

We're in the middle of a civil war [in Iraq] that has cost many American lives, close to 3,000 and almost 25,000 wounded, 50 percent of them grievously; they have been very brave. And sometimes we forget that hundreds of thousands of Iraqis have died — many of them women and children. They're God's children, too.

Somewhere between $300-500 billion has been spent on the war and, as a result, we've created a much more dangerous world. The Iraq Study Group has called the situation grave and deteriorating.

The real enemy was in Afghanistan, yet the Taliban, who harbored Osama Bin Laden, are coming back under Mullah Omar. We don't have enough troops there, and our reconstruction efforts have been badly hindered.

In Iraq, little if any planning was designed for after the invasion. By any objective standard, it has not gone well, and it has siphoned our energies. Remember "mission accomplished" in the spring of 2003? That was a long time ago. And yet, until recently, Democrats have been timid in their criticism of the White House until Jack Murtha seriously questioned the conduct of the war.

Republicans have walked in lockstep behind the president and the media — until no weapons of mass destruction were found.

Our system of checks and balances was not working well because there was little accountability. There has been no effective oversight in Iraq or Afghanistan, but in many other areas as well. Let me give you just one of many egregious examples of how Congress, controlled by the Republicans, ran roughshod over Democrats.

Under the so-called Hastert Rule (named after Speaker of the House Denny Hastert, who was put in power by Tom DeLay), the only bills that could come to the floor were those that had the support of a majority of the Republican caucus. That's not majority rule — that's a travesty. It did great harm to some rock-solid principles of our democracy. This action trampled the rights of Democrats and Republicans alike, and it was strongly supported by the White House. How misguided and very short-sighted. These people lacked an appreciation and understanding of history.

The American people are getting it. And they sent a message this last November 7th that was loud and clear.

They wanted to end partisanship.

They wanted to end incompetence.

They wanted to end the culture of corruption in Washington.

Most of all, they wanted the Iraq war to end, if not immediately, soon. Our presence in Iraq, as the president's own national intelligence estimate has told him, is making things much more dangerous.

The American people want us to address embryonic stem cell research. Stop politicizing science!

The vast majority of Americans want us to do something about budget deficits. The American people have had enough of earmarks — thousands of pet projects that circumvent the regular budgeting process costing billions of dollars to taxpayers — like those bridges from nowhere to nowhere. They're done with sweetheart no-bid contracts awarded to special friends like Halliburton.

These crucial issues present a huge responsibility for the United States as the leading nation in the world today. And we should join in the Kyoto Accords and lead the world in the fight against global warming by weaning ourselves and others away from the addiction to fossil fuels. We must recognize that renewable sources of energy combined with conservation is key not only for us today, but, most importantly, for future generations of Americans.

On these crucial issues, our democracy can and must work effectively, for our children and grandchildren, and on and on and on. We cannot destroy their future or betray their trust. For each of us, that is a goal we must meet.[47]

In a 2011 speech to the Rotary Club of Wilmington, Tom reflects on his approach to politics and courage.

Rotary Club of Wilmington, Delaware
September 29, 2011
By Tom Evans

We need to start listening again to one another — that's the spirit we need to foster throughout the country and indeed the world.

I'll try to cover briefly all the American presidents in the modem era, with some concentration on three with whom I worked closely. There are many lessons learned that are useful in this increasingly polarized time we live in, and there were many similarities and great differences.

All had successes and failures, and all made mistakes. All were concerned with their legacies. All had crises during their tenures. All, to some degree, mistrusted the media and all had a circle-the-wagons mentality, especially in times of crisis.

All, of course, had vice presidents, some of them close, some powerful; most all were qualified, and, in my view, Joe Biden is the best.

All the presidents loved getting away from Washington and most loved to play golf. Some were lucky and some were not. Some endured events over which they had no control that changed the course of their presidencies.

And how their campaigns were conducted is very instructive.

I'll start with Franklin Delano Roosevelt (FDR). No one, other than Lincoln, inherited more difficulties. He was elected during the Great Depression that followed the '29 crash. Millions were out of work — many Americans found themselves wiped out with no safety net to protect them. President Roosevelt moved aggressively and concentrated on jobs, jobs, jobs!

He gave people hope. He established the Civilian Conservation Corps (CCC) and the Works Progress Administration (WPA). They employed huge numbers of workers. In 1935, he established the Social Security Administration, and was criticized for establishing a socialist state. Does that sound familiar?

In 1937, there was a cutback on programs and the economy had a relapse — kind of like not finishing all your antibiotics because you're feeling a little better. (There's certainly a lesson here.) Then came World War II. It was transformational. America came together like never before. Everyone served and everyone sacrificed, whether it was overseas or here at home. Every American played a role in the war effort. We could use that same spirit today with the challenges we face. Five hundred thousand Americans died, but they and their comrades were not forgotten.

After the war, we established the G.I. bill. It built the middle class in America, and was the greatest education program in the history of the world.

We also established the Marshall Plan and, for the first time in history, the victors helped the vanquished. The benefits from these two programs were incalculable, but I wonder if they could have been established in the environment in which we live today. Thank God there were no Tea Parties then, as we looked at the long-term benefits for America and the world. There were some wonderful lessons learned from World War II and the years following.

FDR did a lot for America, as did his successor, Harry Truman. Under Truman's watch, the G.I. bill and the Marshall Plan were enacted.

He also made the courageous decision to drop the atom bomb.

Harry Truman also displayed great courage in firing Douglas McArthur for insubordination, thereby confirming the principal of civilian control over the military. Truman was known for saying the "buck stops here." History has treated him well.

Dwight David Eisenhower was swept into office with widespread popularity in 1952. He might not be nominated by the Republican Party of today. President Eisenhower ended the Korean War and established the interstate highway system. He brought a businessperson's approach to the Oval Office and thought about the needs for the future. It's made a huge difference for the United States — our economy and our national security. Another lasting contribution was his farewell address, where he warned of the military industrial complex.

John Fitzgerald Kennedy took office very young with a young, intelligent and attractive wife, Jackie, and two young children. JFK lifted our spirits, much like President Reagan. He established the Peace Corps, resolved the Cuban missile crisis and utilized our friends and allies to avoid a nuclear confrontation. His biggest failure was not providing promised air cover for the freedom fighters who landed in Cuba, known as the Bay of Pigs fiasco. America's word was brought into question. Is there a lesson here?

Lyndon Baines Johnson loved politics. Americans viewed him as tough and demanding, but effective in getting legislation passed. He ran against Republican Barry Goldwater and won in a landslide.

At the time, the Republican Party was divided. Conservative Republicans were rude and contemptuous of those who disagreed with them, like fellow Republican candidates Nelson Rockefeller and Bill Scranton. It's fair to ask — is history being repeated?

Johnson's campaign focused on the benefits of a series of anti-poverty programs touted as the Great Society, and defeated Goldwater in all but five southern states. However, with Goldwater's rejection of the Civil Rights Act of 1964, the beginning of the southern strategy of the Republican party emerged. Later in life, Sen. Goldwater moderated his views, but his followers did not.

LBJ made tremendous contributions during his time in office. Most notably, he passed the Civil Rights Act, Voting Rights Act, Elementary and Secondary Education Act and Medicare during his tenure.

However, despite the myriad of domestic achievements, escalation of the Vietnam War eclipsed everything else. The notion of guns and butter (domestic initiatives versus military spending) didn't work. Ultimately, the increasingly unpopular war took its toll on Johnson, and he chose not to run for another term. The question was — were our strategic interests so important that it was worth the price we were paying? That's a good question for today.

1968 marked the election of Richard Nixon. After serving as director of economic development in the state of Delaware, I became co-chairman of the Republican National Committee. I even had a White House pass with access to the Situation Room. Nixon had asked me to hit the Democrats hard, but I insisted on accuracy and fairness. To this day, I've always felt that yes, winning is important, but how you play the game is even more important.

Nixon was complex, brilliant, fascinating, and world leaders trusted him. During his time in office, he made tremendous contributions: renewing diplomatic relations with China, establishing the EPA and OSHA and his tremendous support and funding for the National Endowment for the Arts.[48]

The president's resignation created tremendous doubts about the survival of our constitutional system. It's likely Nixon wouldn't get the nomination today. He made a huge mistake in the Watergate cover-up, but historians may yet treat him more kindly. Later on, he and I and John Mitchell developed friendships.

Many were vying to be selected as vice president by President Ford — especially George Bush! I met with Gov. Scranton of Pennsylvania, and he asked me to put in writing my reasons for suggesting Nelson Rockefeller. Ford ultimately did select Rockefeller, and that helped bring stability and confidence to the country. It calmed markets around the world. Much later, in 1992, Bob Woodward, under the Freedom of Information Act, printed my letter of recommendation on the front page of the *Washington Post.*

To his credit, Ford also pardoned Nixon after his loss to Jimmy Carter. Later Nixon and Ford became friends, and that's a good lesson.

President Carter's experience in government was limited, but he was very intelligent. He served as executive officer of the first nuclear sub. While in office, he placed emphasis on the "alleviation of human suffering around the world." He was a quick study but didn't delegate well.

He was unlucky and hurt by our botched rescue effort in Iran, during which helicopters were crippled in a sandstorm. He lost the election to Ronald Reagan because of it, coupled with a bad economy, high unemployment and the unpopular Panama Canal Treaty that ceded control of the Panama Canal.

President Carter has done more after his presidency than virtually any former president. His work in the environment, Habitat for Humanity, human rights, pancreatic cancer research and promotion of fair elections around the globe, is impressive.

Now to Ronald Reagan — good on T.V., great experience as governor, headed Screen Actors Guild, great storyteller, great sense of humor and married to a very influential wife. Ronald Reagan won two elections, both by fairly large margins. But he lost the Iowa caucuses, and his campaign was floundering. I called a meeting of our CORE Group the day after the loss in Iowa. The Core Group was about a dozen of his strongest supporters, including Trent Lott, Carroll Campbell, Henry Hyde, Paul Trible, Bob Walker, Mickey Edwards, et al.

I met with Reagan on a plane from East Orange to Greenville-Spartanburg, S.C. I suggested a change in the appearances he was making. Based on that, he started going out to talk with people after speeches and making himself available to the media. His campaign manager, John Sears, was fired a short time later.

For months, our group had been working very closely with Ed Meese, Dick Allen and others, and we intensified our efforts. We set up task forces on all the major issues. They then became the nucleus of Reagan's policy positions. No one communicated with Congress better than Ronald Reagan, and we set that example in the campaign. Reagan not only gave soaring speeches but he really listened well! Besides ending the Cold War,

President Reagan lifted the spirits of the American people.

George Bush beat Michael Dukakis handily in 1988. He knew world leaders, and they respected him. He built a real coalition in 1991 with Operation Desert Storm in a battle with Iraqi dictator Saddam Hussein.

Despite popularity in the polls due to the victory overseas, he lost the election because of a bad economy. He blamed Alan Greenspan for mismanagement of the Federal Reserve policy. Adding to problems of an eroding economy, the independent candidate Ross Perot siphoned off many votes from the incumbent. In an ironic repeat of history, Ralph Nader, on the Democratic side, gave Bush's son George W. his victory by siphoning off Gore votes in Florida in the 2000 presidential election.

William Jefferson Clinton, a charismatic governor from Arkansas, won in 1992. Initially, he was very unpopular, partly due to his inexperience and Hillary Clinton's push for healthcare reform.

Our economy prospered after Clinton raised taxes. Millions of jobs provided a substantial surplus in U.S. coffers for the first time since 1969, and continued for several years.

I believe his greatest contribution was welfare reform. His policies took away the disincentive to work, which pleased the Republicans. Only a Democratic president working with a Republican majority in Congress could have passed it. It required cooperation. That's a major lesson.

Today, Bill Clinton is arguably one of the most popular living politicians. The Clinton Global Initiative, founded in 2005, convenes leaders to "create and implement solutions to the world's most pressing challenges."

That brings us to the campaign of 2000. The primary between John McCain and George W. Bush may have been the dirtiest I've ever seen. After the South Carolina primary, Karen Hughes, a senior advisor, was asked if Bush would work with McCain. Bush's answer: he lost. We won. End of story. There's a huge lesson here about the need to work together.

In the general election against Al Gore, Gore won by 590,000 votes nationally, but the election came down to Florida. In the debate over whether to do a statewide recount, I was compelled to write an op-ed in the *Washington Post* (included earlier in this book) titled "Count them all again!" The U.S. Supreme Court ultimately ruled in favor of letting the votes stand as originally counted, despite widespread acknowledgment of a different outcome had the state recounted votes. With that decision, George W. Bush became our 43rd president. Although the weeks following the election filled the country with strife and division, his motto became "I'm a uniter not a divider."

After the tragedy on September 11, 2001, Bush had the support of the world. Unfortunately, it was politicized. Huge tax cuts, especially at upper income levels, left an unsustainable budget in place and a widening gap between rich and poor. And due to the almost total lack of regulation, our financial system was on the rocks. The Bush presidency also gave way to the invasion of Iraq and Afghanistan as retribution for the 9/11 attacks, despite no evidence of "weapons of mass destruction" in Iraq at the time.

This eight-year period was filled with a lot of "live for today and don't worry about tomorrow." It was a rather long, gaudy night on the town and, in the clear morning after, we had to pay for our excesses.

In 2008, Barrack Obama was elected. He took over in virtually unprecedented times. I don't believe anyone in history inherited more difficulties — crumbling financial institutions, the car industry on the edge of default, and an economy on the brink of another depression —with the exception of Abraham Lincoln. President Roosevelt also inherited many difficulties, but Democrats and Republicans listened to each other and were willing to cooperate.

That's not the case today, and we are living in extremely difficult times around the globe. Here at home, high unemployment and debt, very little credit available and lack of trust and confidence rule the day. Uncertainty abounds, almost throughout the world. The European debt crisis and problems in other parts of the world plague our own security, plus tremendous competition from other nations, especially India and China.

All of this persists in an atmosphere that is increasingly polarized. Our political system desperately needs reform. Political consultants focus on the negative and instigate conflict instead of relieving it. And we have instantaneous communication with the internet, cable news (24 hours a day) Facebook, YouTube, Bloggers, Twitter, etc., and very little accountability for the accuracy of anything that's said. It's a breeding ground where narrow special interests often prevail.

With all these challenges we face, we do indeed have a wonderful country.

We've faced monumental challenges before. We have an incredible Constitution that gives us the rule of law. And, we are the most generous nation on earth. Think of the Marshall Plan, when our country helped rebuild a broken Europe. Think of the hundreds of thousands of Americans who have given their lives in the cause of freedom. Remember, we may not be perfect, but millions of those outside our shores dream of making America their home.

We will always have conflicts, as our Founding Fathers certainly envisioned. They had some of their own. But there must be respect, cooperation and some degree of compromise! Our system doesn't work without it.[48]

"Trump is not the answer in a democracy"
The News Journal **Delaware Voice**
Monday, August 8, 2016
By Tom Evans

Our Founding Fathers warned us that extreme partisanship would destroy our system of government. Washington, Madison, Adams,

Jefferson, Monroe and Hamilton learned that lesson the hard way. They saw firsthand what happens when a faraway government ignores the will of the people. It is a warning we should heed. Human nature and the way it operates in public life are no different today than in 1776.

Democrats and Republicans disagree sharply on the major issues facing our country. That, in itself, is no surprise. Arguments, even heated ones, are how the people of a boisterous democracy settle things. The give and take of debate strips away the pretense and the posturing. What is left — the real differences — very often lead the way to compromise. Yet that only works when all sides see their opponents as fellow Americans.

That is not the case today. Polarization is probably greater than at almost any time in our history, with the exception of the years leading up to the Civil War. There are too few working for compromise and far too few who respect those on opposing sides.

And that is dangerous. This lack of respect has spread beyond opponents or public officials. It has grown into a festering disrespect of public office, even toward the presidency itself.

We have had strong disagreements between our two major parties, but, in times of danger, Republicans and Democrats have always come together. We have always had candidates for president from each party — winner or loser — who accepted and respected our constitutional system.

Just before America joined our allies in World War II, President Franklin Roosevelt, a Democrat, faced Wendell Willkie, a Republican, in the 1940 presidential campaign. Roosevelt won. In 1944, Gov. Dewey of New York lost to Roosevelt despite the demonization of FDR and the New Deal.

In 1946, just after the end of the war, voters tired of the ruling Democratic Party. Republicans recaptured control of the U.S. House and Senate for the first time since 1932. In 1948, the Republican Gov. Thomas Dewey of New York was heavily favored to beat President Harry Truman, yet Truman pulled off one of the greatest upsets in presidential history.

However, during the years after World War II, Democrats and Republicans worked together to pass two major bills in 1948, the GI Bill and the Marshall Plan. The G.I. bill helped substantially in building the middle class in America, while the Marshall Plan rebuilt the economies of our former foes, the first time in history when the victor helped the vanquished. Both of these bills helped America.

In every one of these races and most throughout our history, the major parties offered candidates who, regardless of political outlook, saw themselves as part of our constitutional system.

This is not the situation today. We are close to ignoring that warning from the Founding Fathers against extreme partisanship. That would be foolish in any age, but in today's threatening environment, that attitude is suicidal.

Start with the most obvious threat: radical Islamic terrorism (we cannot even agree on what to call it). Radical tensions, the economy, gun violence, climate change and the inevitable sea rise that follows.

These problems are not going away, and many wonder if our political system is up to the task. The system developed by Washington, Madison and others has been usurped by talking heads and Twitter blasts.

Leadership is needed to help us heal our wounds.

That is not the choice before us.

Never before has a candidate of one of our major political parties been so divisive. Donald Trump is unqualified to lead our country on any basis used. His lack of public service, of humility, of understanding issues like climate change and foreign policy, should disqualify him. He lacks what it takes to lead this country.

Clearly a President Trump would be dangerous for America and the rest of the world.

The closest he comes to consistent policy is his belligerence toward people who disagree with him.[49]

QUALITIES OF A PRESIDENT

Tom compiled a list of presidential qualities prior to the 2008 presidential election that highlighted prudent characteristics and experience needed for leading our nation. They are an informative measuring stick to hold to candidates of both parties.

♦ A person with intellect who understands and appreciates history.

♦ Someone who can truly be a uniter and not a divider.

♦ Someone who respects our Constitution and the rule of law it established.

♦ Someone who listens to others and appreciates their views.

♦ Someone who has traveled widely and understands the culture of other regions and nations. Ideally, they will have developed relationships with leaders in other nations.

♦ Someone who can speak well and inspire others, especially younger Americans.

♦ Someone who speaks honestly. Ideally, someone who understands government so that they can deal effectively with the bureaucracy.

♦ Someone who can work well with others and who has demonstrated an ability to manage well.

♦ Someone who will attract outstanding and dedicated people to government — someone who would use Sandra Day O'Connor as their model for appointments to the Supreme Court, not Clarence Thomas.

♦ Someone who cares for all God's creatures and understands that sound economic policy and good environmental policies are not competing values — they are not mutually exclusive. The next president must address the global warming issue!

- Someone who has demonstrated personal generosity and kindness to others.

- Someone who believes in our free enterprise system, but who also believes in caring for those in need and the crying need to recognize that the widening gap between rich and poor in our country and around the world is a very pressing issue.

- Someone who recognizes the importance of education in our increasingly competitive world.

- Someone who will promote innovation in every field.

- Someone who believes in a higher power.

- Someone who recognizes and will implement plans to develop alternative sources of energy and who recognizes the importance of conservation.

- Someone who understands the need to be strong militarily, but who understands that diplomacy can also be important. Someone with more humility than swagger, who will command respect from the rest of the world. And that means someone who cares about how we are perceived. We need respect not because of our military strength, but because of our values.

♦ Someone who is committed to winning but is just as committed to playing the game fairly.

♦ Someone who recognizes that we have a duty to future generations of Americans, i.e., the budget deficit.

Among the myriad of notes he's kept over the years, this passage sums up his continued optimism for the future. "America is still the land of opportunity and hope. We are a beacon of freedom for all the world to see. A crucial part of freedom is the ability to speak out. It has set us apart for many years. We should encourage diversity of thought and we should respect one another. There is too much polarization, and those flickers of disagreement are being fanned into flames by political consultants and lobbyists. But we will survive them. We have problems, but our country is still a great hope for mankind."

PART IV

CHARACTER

CHAPTER SIXTEEN

COMMITMENT, FAITH, AND FORGIVENESS

As highlighted previously, Tom spoke at many events — in Congress, at clubs, universities, eulogies and prayer breakfasts. While Tom was in Congress in the late 1970s, he was invited to speak at the Governor's Prayer Breakfast in Oregon by Doug Coe, associate director of The Fellowship, the organization that coordinated the prayer breakfasts, and by Mark Hatfield, governor of Oregon. Tom accepted.

Unfortunately, many votes were scheduled in the House the night before the early morning event. Not one to disappoint, instead of canceling the engagement, he rescheduled the flight arrangements. After a long night at the Capitol, he booked a midnight flight from D.C. to Atlanta and from Atlanta to Seattle, followed by another leg into Oregon. The final drive left Tom with just enough time to shower in the gym at Willamette University in Salem before arriving at the 8 a.m. Prayer Breakfast. As he rose to speak, the attendees greeted him with cheers of appreciation for his efforts. He made the commitment and was determined to meet it and made people feel they were worth the effort. And, he's sure that message resonated with them more than even the wisest words in his speech that day.

Prayer breakfasts serve to create unity between left and right and those of different backgrounds. National Prayer Breakfasts have included dignitaries from around the globe and have been attended by every president since Dwight Eisenhower. The breakfasts now cast a wider net and are attended by those with faiths other than Christianity. Although some see it as an opportunity to bring people together, it also serves a political purpose to gain access to the political leaders without being vetted in the usual governmental hierarchy.[50]

Doug Coe also asked Tom to speak at a prayer breakfast in Bermuda in the late 1970s, a time of great upheaval in the small island country and British territory. In 1977, racial riots plagued the country between the ruling white minority and a long-oppressed Black majority. Although full voting rights were granted to Blacks in 1963, discriminatory barriers remained. Tom spoke at a time of intense racial tension.[51]

His purpose was to bring people together and end the hostility. He shared his values with the group — work together and respect each other. "We are all God's children." He continued, "If we can be one in spirit, we can live together in a bond of peace." Coe knew he delivered the right messenger for that turbulent time.

Tom also delivered a speech at the National Prayer Breakfast in February of 1981, just after Ronald Reagan's first inauguration. As a newcomer to the prayer breakfast, Reagan sought Tom's counsel to find out who would be there and what to say. He then drove with Reagan to the event.

Years later, Tom received an invitation to attend a small dinner before the Governor's Prayer Breakfast in Dover, Del., by Dick Murchinson, a good friend who served as Tom's deputy at the Delaware State Development Department in the late 60s. Murchinson noted that Chuck Colson was the featured speaker at the event.

Chuck Colson served as special counsel to President Nixon and went to jail for his misdeeds during the Watergate scandal. During his time serving the president, Colson was less than respectful to Tom and sought to get Nixon to fire him.

But Tom didn't want to embarrass Colson by attending and considered refusing his colleague's invitation. Then, Mary Page told him, "I think he's changed."

While Colson was in jail, he founded Prison Fellowship that "exists to serve all those affected by crime and incarceration." Tom reconsidered and accepted.[52]

Upon arrival at the governor's mansion, Tom saw Colson standing at the other end of a long, wide hallway. Colson walked toward him, arms wide open, and embraced Tom. "Please forgive me for what I tried to do to you."

Tom said, "I forgave you long ago."

Tom's Christian faith serves as his guiding compass when dealing with people and issues, like wildlife and the environment. "We need to care for those who have no voice." And, he uses his voice, whether with a megaphone or pen, to move people. He also believes in the power of forgiveness.

That forgiveness extends to his family as well. When his daughter Page was 14, she "borrowed" the family car without permission. She may have gotten away with it except she crossed paths with her mother driving down the road in her Impala station wagon. Mary Page slammed on the brakes and pointed, "You get your butt home right now!"

Feeling the full wrath from her mother at that moment, Page was sent in to get the same from her father. Instead, he said, "Well, I know what a good driver you are, Pagie." And then he paused. "But it's the other drivers I'm worried about."

Page acknowledges he should not have let her off the hook that easily, but this was an example of how forgiving — and trusting — her dad is as a father. When it comes to unconditional love, Tom gives that in spades — to all three of his children. And now, he gives it to his three grandchildren. He is the go-to guy when you need advice or encouragement.

Page also describes her dad as "generous to a fault. But that's a pretty good fault to have."

CHAPTER SEVENTEEN

COURAGE AND RISK-TAKING

Much of Tom's work could not have happened without taking a few risks to get things done. He wasn't afraid of facing them head on. His proclivity for heading into the risk instead of shying from it revealed itself even as a young boy.

At age five, his father took the training wheels off his bike, pushed him 30 feet, and then Tom took off down the street solo — wind blowing through his hair and heart pounding with the thrill of freedom captured in that moment. It was the same boy who took the family's small boat too far down the Nanticoke river just to see where he'd end up.

He loves the thrill of competition. It was the same young man who emerged victorious on the wrestling mat, and the man who still loves to gather a foursome for a round at the links — always looking to come out with the low score on his card.

As the Outreach Committee chairman at Christ Church in the 60s, Tom shook things up from the old way of operating. The committee was charged with raising funds and distributing their substantial resources to local organizations that served the community.

Prior to Tom joining the committee, funds were dispersed to tried and true organizations — those already supported by the United Way. As the chairman of the committee, he sought new and innovative organizations, many of which had admirable visions but no track record of success. The committee pushed the church to invest in lesser-known groups hoping they might find one that changed the way Wilmington served those that needed it most. Some projects were successful, and some were not. But Tom didn't back down from the quest.

Ed O'Donnell, a member of the committee, said of him, "He loves and respects people. He is non-judgmental and doesn't look for the bad in people." It was with that attitude Tom trusted in people and organizations that had no record of success. If an organization's mission was to help those in need, he was willing to take a chance and applaud them for their good work in the community.

Nor did he shy away from asking things of others. In the 60s, he invited famous golfers Arnold Palmer and Jack Nicholas to participate in charity golf tournaments and then strolled down the fairway with each. He solicited countless people to support the causes and candidates he believed in. He never demanded things of people but had a way of bringing them to his side by making them feel part of the solution. Just as he was asked to give of himself with time and treasure, he never shied away from asking others because it was too hard or too uncomfortable. Tom risked a lot of no's but more often got to yes.

In 1979, the scene played out at the Delaware Theatre Company's first play, staged in an old firehouse in Wilmington, Delaware. Tom and Mary Page attended the opening with fellow artist Catharina Baart and her husband, Livingston Biddle, a prominent Philadelphian and head of the National Endowment for the Arts.

The theater showed great promise yet lacked funding, a problem most theater communities face. Tom wasted no time asking for support for the fledging theater, not only for the funding but for the status national funding brought to attract new patrons and donors.

The hiccup arose because of timing. The NEA fiscal year ended four days prior to the premiere and four days too late for the funding and recognition Tom was seeking because no line item for the theater existed in the new budget. A year is a lifetime away for small theaters hoping to survive.

A wry smile appears on Tom's face when he recounts the story: the men jokingly made a pact to go to jail together if it was found out that the check was pre-dated. Would another man have taken that risk for an organization that didn't serve him personally, other than the enjoyment of a good show?

Tom's story with Livingston, whom he fondly called Livi, continued into the next decade. President Reagan's 1981 budget slashed funding for the NEA by an unimaginable 50 percent. Besides supporting arts in his community, Tom believed in the power of the arts to cultivate a thriving society, rich in beauty and culture. He supported Mary Page as a well-respected artist. He supported the community that surrounded her, not just for her, but because of the importance of fostering creative expression in wide-ranging artistic endeavors and the benefits to society that come from bringing that work to life. He saw, firsthand, how a strong arts presence enriched the community.

Tom testified before the House in support of lesser cuts or restructuring how and when the cuts were implemented. With an impassioned plea, Tom cited the far-reaching detrimental effects on the artistic community if organizations were not given time to find other funding sources if there were any. He asked David Stockman, chairman of the Office of Management and Budget, to reconsider what Tom considered an ill-advised cut to a popular and valuable organization. As a result, a large portion of the NEA funding was restored to the budget. He gained allies on the Democratic side of the aisle for his efforts.

In 1981, Tom flew into headwinds when he also tried to stop budget cuts to the EXIM Bank. With deficit hawks circling the excesses in an ever-ballooning list of domestic and foreign priorities, the Export-Import Bank took its place at the monetary guillotine.

Tom opposed proposed cuts to the bank. Although he and his Republican colleagues would have preferred elimination of all interference in international business negotiation, he felt that without assistance from the government, U.S. companies couldn't fairly compete in the world marketplace.

In a July 5 *Washington Star* opinion piece, he stated, "A careful analysis of the facts leads to the conclusion that unilateral reductions in EXIM Bank's lending ability will subvert our competitive export position, worsen our balance of trade, undermine any possibility of reaching a binding international agreement on credit practices, and have little or no impact on the federal budget ."[53]

Despite his plea, EXIM Bank's budget was cut.

Not willing to accept defeat on the issue, Tom worked even harder that night into the next day to rectify the decision. Recognizing the complexity of the bank's objectives, he sought to educate and persuade his colleagues about the benefits of the bank's impact, not just to major corporations, but to the suppliers and employees who depended on them. He rallied congress to reverse its decision the next day. That kind of courage and tenacity is a rare find in today's political world.

The thrill-seeking also brought him to the racetrack. He loves to play the ponies at his home tracks, Delaware Park in Newark and Gulf Stream Park in Florida, watching with rapt anticipation for his horse to cross the finish line. His love of the sport also brought him to the famed Kentucky Derby in Louisville for many years.

Prior to the Florida Derby in Hallandale Beach, Fla. at Gulfstream Park in 1997, Tom bought a small ownership of a promising racehorse. Captain Bodgit ran in the Grade 1 race that year but was not favored. Although he watched the race via simulcast, his son made it just in time to place a win bet at the track. The great Captain beat the favorite and won the Florida Derby going away. Several hours later, Tom received a collect call. The operator said, "You have a collect call from Captain Bodgit." Tom and Mary Page could not have been happier and, of course, accepted the call.

Speaking about the race, Tom said, "When he got halfway down the stretch with the lead, I was up and cheering. I can't tell you how great a feeling that was!"[54] Captain Bodgit went on to win the Wood Memorial at Aqueduct later that year. The thrill was hard to beat.

Tom and Mary Page packed their bags for the Kentucky Derby in Louisville for a potentially historic event. The day before Captain Bodgit was to run, the couple attended the Kentucky Oaks, a long-established race for three-year-old fillies. A prominent piece in the *Daily Racing Form* featured a story about Tom — his partial ownership of Captain Bodgit and his seat years prior in the U.S. House of Representatives — a combination not often seen. "Years of going to the races and enjoying many great times at Derbys past could never prepare you for this incredible moment played out in two electrifying minutes in arguably the greatest classic in American sports. From my own perspective, the anxiety that accompanies political campaigning cannot compare with the anxiety you feel in the days, hours and minutes leading up to the Kentucky Derby," Tom said in the article.

His horse was the favorite at the Kentucky Derby in 1997 but fell short by a head behind Silver Charm. Captain Bodgit retired due to injury later that year, but Tom's memory of the experience still brings a smile to his face.

Although Captain Bodgit didn't win, Tom didn't leave empty-handed. He snapped a photo with actress Bo Derek (of the movie *10*) and her sister.

He didn't stop with the love of the action at the track. Tom spoke out in support of horse racing, and specifically of Delaware state laws in support of Delaware Park, citing the importance to the Delaware economy. While hundreds of jobs were at stake at the racetrack itself, from ticket-takers to stable workers, thousands in the surrounding Delaware community counted on racing for their jobs, as well as valuable revenue to fill state government coffers.

Tom stands between actress Bo Derek and her sister Carey at the Kentucky Derby.

Tom still enjoys his morning and late-day chats with his financial brokers to discuss prospects for individual stocks and the financial markets in general. The thrill of the game gets him as energized each morning as his steaming cup of coffee. Although his decisions in the market, especially during volatile times, have sometimes left him vulnerable, he still prefers the excitement of the opening and closing bells to a more measured approach.

As the previous chapters have demonstrated, Tom isn't afraid to speak his mind. As a public figure, any stance can bring admiration or ire, or both at the same time. Especially as a moderate Republican, his position on issues cross traditional lines of left and right, leaving him in the crosshairs of criticism. But he doesn't shy away or back down regardless of possible consequences.

For politicians who measure every word so as not to agitate party leaders and for citizens, who remain quiet for fear of public rejection or criticism, Tom encourages all to take a risk — to speak out for what is right.

The reward for courage is far greater than any regret for standing up and speaking truth to power.

CONCLUSION

Tom is admittedly a man of privilege. His admittance into the Society of the Cincinnati, America's oldest patriotic association, testifies to a family heritage stretching back to the roots of our country's independence. Access to an excellent education, positive role models, and private golf courses opened doors and catapulted him into a world of influence and power most will never experience.

What makes Tom's story remarkable is what he did — and still does — with that privilege. Passion and enthusiasm are the lenses through which he operates. His tireless work ethic paired with a golden heart led to a life filled with meaningful accomplishments in politics, for the environment, and for causes that have been fortunate enough to have his support.

Conclusion

His life is filled with gratitude — for the people, opportunities, and gifts he's been given. No one is more grateful for his family and the countless friends, colleagues, and acquaintances who crisscrossed his life than Tom. The coalitions he formed were a result of his good nature and acknowledgment that people need to come together to accomplish great things. No one can do it all on their own.

Tom can straddle the line between left and right and engage people in the middle regardless of the times. He found and still finds the win-win in situations where everyone walks away feeling like they've gained more than they've lost. It's a trait he admires in Joe Biden. It's what the country needs during this tenuous time in history. And, it's hard to come by in politics.

The power of bipartisanship is evident in the letters he's received over the years from Democrats and Republicans. A note from Democrat Berkley Bedell read, "One of my proudest acts during my 12 years in Congress was my cutting a tape endorsing you for re-election, even though you were a Republican and I was a Democrat." Democrat Sam Shipley, who Tom defeated in his first election victory, said of Tom in an article in *The News Journal*, "He's a guy of substance."[55] Even the liberal political voice of the *New York Times*, John Oakes, penned a note of appreciation to Tom for his courage on environmental legislation in Congress.

He's proud of the work he's done and considers his accomplishments of value to future generations not only for the legislation passed but for the manner in which it was accomplished. He sees the cooperation he engendered as a model for politicians and citizens alike. It's a way of being, not just doing.

The measure of a successful politician today is to closely tether yourself to party above people and loyalty above country. And while he doesn't hark back to the "glory days" in politics, he is maddened by the partisan divide so wide as not to do the people's work at all. While it sometimes seems impossible to find a way out of the chasm, he believes that voters have a choice to elect a person to bring the country together, heal the wounds of divisiveness, and lead the nation into a better, more just future.

He's come a long way from supporting Goldwater and the most conservative factions of the Republican party. Or, maybe it was that the party moved to the right without him. Either way, the long-time Republican finds himself more closely aligned with key Democratic values: equality and fairness in human relations and protection of the environment, including all its inhabitants.

As a spiritual man, he believes that the environment, the earth and all its creatures were bequeathed to humanity to cherish, preserve and protect. Honoring the interdependent web of all existence is a moral obligation and one for each person to act upon through independent action, advocacy, and casting a ballot at the voting booth.

Tom embodies a life filled with joy for the work he's done and for the people who've graced it. Mostly, the joy is for the mark he leaves on history and a life's purpose fulfilled.

Much of his passion for his environmental work is about saving the earth for future generations. "I want this earth to be a better place for my children, my grandchildren, and my grandchildren's children. The future depends on everyone working together. The earth knows no political boundaries."

Conclusion

"Our destiny doesn't lie in bringing people down to some common standard, but rather by giving everyone an opportunity to move up to their highest potential."

~ Tom Evans

APPENDIX

Tom's resume is varied and impressive. His work and leadership started at an early age and continues today. It would have been impossible to share all that he's done in his 89-plus years in this book. To fill in the gaps not shared, his resume speaks to a life well-lived and how his impact on history will endure.

THOMAS B. EVANS'S RESUME

Education

University of Virginia (B.A. and LLB)

President of St. Elmo Hall and member and officer of a number of organizations at the University of Virginia, including the Student Council and Inter-Fraternity Council. Member of the IMP Society where members elected him "king."

Personal

Married to Mary Page (Hilliard) Evans, a well-known and accomplished artist; three children — Thomas B. Evans, III, Robert Speir Evans, Page Evans Corey, and three grandchildren Peyton, Sam and Katherine.

Business and Professional

Chairman of the Evans Group, Ltd., a Washington, D.C.-based consulting firm; member of the Virginia State Bar.

Former head of an insurance-consulting firm specializing in employee benefit plans; former member of the board of World Wide Minerals (WWM), a Canadian company with uranium mining interests in Mongolia and Kazakhstan; former member of the board of Zemex Corporation (listed on the NYSE) and a member of the company's audit committee; former member of the board of the Federal Home Loan Bank of Pittsburgh, Artesian Water Company, Chronar Corporation (a solar energy company) and Juno

Limited, a Bermuda-based company focusing on trade and investment in China.

Former partner in the law firm of O'Connor & Hannan and co-managing partner of the firm of Manatt, Phelps, Rothenberg & Evans. As chairman of the legislative committees at both law firms, he coordinated activities on behalf of clients. As a director of WWM, took the lead in efforts to recover investments made in a de facto nationalized uranium mine in Kazakhstan. As a director of Zemex, he was actively involved in many of the company's operations, including marketing, acquisitions and financing (including service on a committee of the board working closely with investment bankers and others).

International Experience

Tom Evans has represented a number of countries, often working directly with presidents and prime ministers. He has set up numerous meetings for foreign leaders with Administration officials, Members of Congress, think tanks and the media and has played a key role in having legislation enacted strengthening ties between these countries and the United States. The foreign clients represented include Cyprus, Romania, the Kazakhstan 21st Century Foundation (which supports the principal opposition party in Kazakhstan), Jamaica, Sudan, Nigeria and Taiwan. He has also represented corporations, including NEC and Naigai, both Japanese companies, and Unideal-Navitankers of Greece.

For Cyprus, he generated widespread support in Congress for a U.S. role in ending the Turkish occupation of Northern Cyprus, reuniting Cyprus and providing financial aid for projects benefitting both the Greek and Turkish Cypriot communities. In the process, he helped in drafting legislation, congressional resolutions and floor statements, op-ed articles and editorials. He also organized rallies, think-tank meetings and congressional hearings.

He led a successful effort in the U.S. Congress to provide Romania with normal trade status despite substantial congressional opposition. Also played a key role in enhancing U.S. support for Romania's entry into NATO. He developed strong congressional support for efforts by the Kazakhstan 21st Century Foundation to bring democracy, a free press, and respect for human rights to Kazakhstan. Most especially, he generated awareness in both the Congress and the administration of the danger that continued repression in Kazakhstan could strengthen Islamic extremists.

For Jamaica, he was instrumental in obtaining tens of millions of dollars in U.S. foreign assistance. He also assisted in negotiations with the World Bank and the International Monetary Fund. As a former member of Congress, he represented the United States at the country's celebration of its twentieth anniversary of independence. For Sudan, he helped to secure U.S. foreign assistance and worked directly with President Jaafar Numeiri to promote Muslim-Christian reconciliation. He assisted Nigeria in restructuring its foreign debt and worked with U.S. and Nigerian officials to interdict drug trafficking from Nigeria to the U.S. He also worked to expand the number of countries according diplomatic recognition to Taiwan as the Republic of China.

He introduced the president of Naigai, a Japanese manufacturer of specialty scientific glass, to key U.S. officials, including the U.S. ambassador to Japan, in a successful effort to generate U.S. pressure on the Japanese government to stop Japanese companies from illegally retaliating against Naigai for obtaining some of its raw material requirements from the U.S. After years of futile effort, Unideal-Navitanker, a Greek shipping company, turned to Tom Evans to resolve problems with the U.S. Maritime Administration. As a result, bonding requirements were cut in half and a prohibition against using former U.S. flag vessels in certain trade was lifted.

Tom Evans served in Congress as the ranking Republican on the International Financial Institutions Subcommittee of the House Banking Committee. He acted as the Republican floor leader for legislation funding organizations like the World Bank.

Domestic Clients

In addition to international clients, Tom Evans has successfully represented a diverse group of domestic clients. They include American Airlines, TIAA-CREF (the giant pension fund), Matlack, Inc., Aventis Behring Pharmaceutical Co., a coalition of savings and loan associations, Rollins Environmental Services, and Riddell Sports.

In a matter critical to the future of Rollins Environmental Services, Tom Evans persuaded the EPA to cancel a preliminary permit for Waste Management Inc. to burn toxic waste in the Gulf of Mexico. Without this effort, Rollins would have been driven out of business, since its incinerators were land-based and subject to higher environmental standards and hence more expensive for customers.

In a related issue involving a coalition of land-based incinerators of toxic waste in addition to

Rollins, all of which were held to high Clean Air Act standards, he successfully fought the cement industry, which was burning toxic waste in kilns with limited regulation. A bill considered by the House Appropriations Committee and reported out of that committee for a vote on the floor would have prevented the EPA from exercising tighter control over cement kilns burning toxic waste. Tom Evans played a prominent role in defeating that provision.

In the case of Matlack, Inc. (Pipeline on Wheels), Tom Evans secured regulations that made this trucking firm more competitive. For Aventis Behring, he secured millions of dollars in research grants from the Department of Defense.

During congressional consideration of the Financial Institutions Reform, Recovery and Enforcement Act, he helped to win the only victory achieved by a coalition of beleaguered savings and loan associations. His initiative, as the leader of a coalition of law and lobbying firms working on behalf of S&L's, permitted mortgage servicing rights to be included in the counting of capital by the regulators, thus permitting some S&L's to remain in business.

Whether working on behalf of coalitions or individual companies, Tom Evans often structures his efforts like national political campaigns. For example, in the effort described earlier to stop the incineration of toxic waste at sea, he mobilized a number of organizations and individuals, including environmental groups, tourist and health-related organizations and the media, to bring attention to the issue. As a result, he was successful in reversing a preliminary EPA decision to permit incineration at sea. He used the same approach in bringing attention to the dangers inherent in burning toxic waste in land-based cement kilns, defeating very powerful and entrenched interests in the process. He has successfully used the same technique in initiatives to promote human rights and other causes.

Public Service

Member of the U.S. House of Representatives 1977—1983; member of the Republican Leadership in the House in 1981 and 1982; chairman-elect of the Environmental and Energy Study Conference; vice chairman and chairman-elect of the Arts Caucus; member of House Banking Committee and the Merchant Marine and Fisheries Committee 1977—1983. Served as a congressional delegate to the U.N. Law of the Sea Conference.

Former director of the Delaware State Development Department. Established the first Jobs Development Bank, which matched job openings with job applicants in Delaware. The program also included the hiring of young people for summer jobs where they were supervised and where there were incentive awards for attendance, attitude and work performed. It became a model for the nation. Served as a member of the Governor's Council on Vocational Education and as the first member of the Governor's Council on Marine and Coastal Affairs. The first Coastal Zone

Management Program in the nation stemmed from the Coastal Affairs Council.

Major Legislative Accomplishments

Author of the Coastal Barrier Resources Act; co-sponsor and Republican floor leader for the Alaska Lands Act; Republican floor leader for U.S. funding for multilateral development institutions such as the World Bank; de facto Republican leader for the Chrysler assistance bill; preserved funding for the National Endowment for the Arts as well as funding for organizations involved in assisting the handicapped; preserved funding for the Export-Import Bank; the only member of Congress to speak against minting of the Susan B. Anthony dollar coin, which later proved to be unpopular and was eventually withdrawn from circulation.

Author of an amendment conditioning Export-Import Bank assistance on U.S. companies' support for equal rights and opportunities for all employees in the companies' South Africa operations; successfully headed a congressional coalition to eliminate funding for pork-barrel projects in order to reduce the budget deficit; co-author of the first anti-dumping act to protect the Delaware, Maryland and New Jersey coastlines.

Accomplishments for Delaware

Secured funding for the rehabilitation of the Wilmington train station; secured funding for moderate- and low-income housing, senior citizen housing and housing for the handicapped; provided funding for senior citizen transportation. After legislation was passed in the U.S. Senate that would have essentially scuttled the Dover Air Force Base, Tom Evans was a key leader of a coalition of House members that successfully turned the vote around and preserved thousands of jobs and essential functions for the Air Force. Successfully pressed for the rehabilitation of the Delmarva Rail Lines; assisted in funding for the Augustine Bridge and for access to and from U.S. Route 95 at a critical point in Delaware; provided funding to improve navigational aids in the Delaware River and Bay.

Provided funding to expand Delaware Technical and Community College and to build a major center at Lewes for the University of Delaware's College of Marine Studies; saved the historic Fenwick Island Lighthouse; provided funding for many other projects of a smaller nature throughout Delaware, such as senior citizen centers, water resource projects and community centers. As chairman of the Outreach Committee at Christ Church, initiated funding and otherwise assisted high-risk programs in Delaware, such as alcohol rehabilitation, long before other organizations, such as the United Way, provided assistance. Assisted hundreds and probably thousands of Delawareans with individual problems, particularly in dealing with the Washington bureaucracy.

Publications

Numerous op-ed articles in publications such as *The Christian Science Monitor, The Washington Post, The Washington Times, The Philadelphia*

Inquirer, The Hartford Courant, Orlando Sentinel and Star and others in Florida.

Awards and Recognition

Tom Evans' national honors include the American Legion Award for Employment of the Handicapped; the Charles Bonner Award for Initiatives in Boating Safety; and environmental awards from Americans for the Coast, the Sierra Club, National Wildlife Federation and the Environmental and Energy Conference of the Congress. He is also a recipient of an award from the Coalition of Peace Through Strength for his national security leadership. Most recently, he was awarded the Medal of Merit by The Garden Club of America for his longstanding devotion to conservation.

Tom Evans continues to give addresses to major groups. Speeches have included addresses at the University of Delaware, the University of Delaware's Academy of Lifelong Learning, Georgetown University, the American Center in Moscow and a series of lectures at Florida Atlantic

University's Lifelong Learning Society in 2005. He also gave the initial address in the fall from 2004-2007 as a part of Florida Atlantic University's Distinguished Speaker Series. Other participants in the series included two individuals who were nominees of their party for president of the United States.

Pro Bono Activities

Tom Evans was a member of the Children' s Hearing and Speech Center, the Alaska Wilderness League and the Coast Alliance. The latter two organizations produce research and policy papers related to the environment. They also lobby the Congress and the administration. Tom Evans took the lead on lobbying for the Coast Alliance, whose board consists of representatives from most of the national environmental groups. As one of 14 board members of the Alaska Wilderness League, he took an active role in protecting some of Alaska's great treasures. That organization has taken the lead in protecting the Arctic National Wildlife Refuge.

Appendix

Tom Evans is an honorary life member of the board of the Delaware chapter of the American Red Cross; former member of the board and chairman of special gifts for the Delaware chapter of the Red Cross; formerly an active fundraiser for the United Way; chairman in Delaware for the United Negro College Fund and Radio Free Europe/Radio Liberty; former member of the Executive Committee and Board of Trustees of Wesley College in Dover, Del.; former member of the Board of Trustees of Woodberry Forest School in Orange, Va.; emeritus member of the College Board of Trustees at the University of Virginia (now called the College Foundation); former member of the executive committee and member of the board of the Environmental and Energy Study Institute, which produces research papers on environmental issues; former member of the Board of Trustees of Ford's Theatre in Washington.

Political

Former co-chairman and chief operating officer of the Republican National Committee; past

Republican national committeeman from Delaware and member of the executive committee of the Republican National Committee; former deputy chairman and member of the executive committee of the Republican National Finance Committee; former chairman of the Nixon for President Committee in Delaware and regional finance chairman (eleven states) of the Nixon presidential campaign; chairman of the Congressional Steering Committee for Reagan-Bush in 1980 and member of the executive committee of that campaign; served briefly in the Reagan "kitchen cabinet"; vice chairman of the Advisory Board for the 1984 Reagan-Bush campaign and fundraiser for many presidential campaigns.

Tom Evans served on the fundraising steering committees for many members of Congress. He was vice chairman and member of the executive committee of the National Congressional Campaign Committee (principal liaison to the White House); delegate to a number of Republican

Appendix

national conventions and a speaker at three of
them, including giving the primary seconding
speech for Ronald Reagan in 1980 and a seconding
speech for Gerald Ford in 1976. Tom Evans speaks
on the environment, human rights and politics. He
is the recipient of a number of political honors
including the Middlesex County, Mass., Lincoln
award. Recipients have included Richard Nixon,
Gerald Ford, Trent Lott, Bob Dole and Jack Kemp.

Sports

Former captain of the University of Virginia golf
team and member of the university's track team.
Sports enthusiast, skier and golfer; has
participated in the National Amateur Golf
championships; won a number of golf
tournaments, including four club championships;
past president of the Delaware State Golf
Association and member of the executive
committee of the Philadelphia Golf Association;
chairman of two major fundraising events, which
included participation by golfers Jack Nicklaus,
Arnold Palmer and Gary Player; co-chairman of

the committee in charge of the National Amateur played at the Wilmington Country Club. Tom Evans is also a member of the United States Seniors' Golf Association.

Club Memberships

Honorary member of Pine Valley Golf Club, member of the Wilmington Country Club, St. Andrews Club and the Gulf Stream Golf Club. Member of Chowder and Marching Club in Congress, which holds weekly meetings and consists of members of the Republican leadership in the House and Senate, including the Speaker of the House and Republican leaders in the Senate.

PHOTOS

These photos represent just a handful of the thousands of memories captured on film. The people and events shown are cherished friends, colleagues and family members from Tom's home state of Delaware and around the world.

Arnold Palmer tees off at a 1963 charity golf tournament in Wilmington, Del., with Tom and the rest of the foursome proceeding to the first hole.

With Tom discussing the building of the University of
Delaware's College of Marine Studies are Bill Gaither, the
college's first dean, and Rep. Pete McCloskey, member of
the Merchant Marine and Fisheries Committee who
supported funding for the project.

Ellis Taylor, former head of Artesian Water and nine-time
winner of the Delaware Amateur Golf Tournament, is
seated next to Tom at an Artesian board meeting.

This photo of President Nixon with Mary Page, son Rob, and
daughter Page appeared in newspapers around the world. Mary
Page untangled Page's hair from the president's coat button
after the Evans family posed for a photo with Nixon.

Tom with Republican leader John Rhodes and Gov. Reagan
in a private meeting before the Republican National
Convention in Detroit in 1980.

Tom walking President-Elect Reagan from the Senate to meet members of the House with Paul Laxalt and Lynn Nofzinger following behind.

Nancy and President Reagan welcoming Mary Page and Tom at a reception for the CORE group.

Tom meeting with House Speaker Tip O'Neill, Tom
Korologos, Jim Baker and Ed Meese.

Tom in a meeting in the Oval Office with President Reagan.

Mary Page with Vice President George Bush at a campaign
event for Tom.

George and Barbara Bush campaigning for Tom with
daughter Page and her friends.

Sen. Bob Dole stumping for Tom at a campaign rally in
Delaware.

Tom presenting a baseball bat signed and given to the
president by all-star Phillies pitcher Steve Carlton.

Nancy Reagan lighting the president's cake for his 70th
birthday. Tom is joined by House Speaker Tip O'Neill, Paul
Laxalt, and Bob Michel.

A light moment at a Democratic and Republican leadership
meeting in the speaker's office with Reagan and Bush.

Tom sharing a laugh with President Reagan.

Tom with President Gaafar Nimeiry of Sudan and Sudanese
Ambassador to the U.S. Omar Eissa at a party at the
Sudanese Embassy.

Tom with the President Glafcos Clerides of Cyprus and
Ambassador Andrew Jacovides.

Ambassador J. Clifford Folger with former Reagan
campaign chair Bill Casey and Tom.

Tom receives a warm greeting from Congressman Jack
Kemp of New York.

Tom giving a speech at the Amtrak Shops in Wilmington,
Del., promising to fight relocation to another state. His
stance won him favor with the union.

Tom with Delaware businessman and friend Jim Gilliam.

Gene Bunting, Tom and Gov. Russ Peterson.

Tom with friends Peg and Laird Stabler.

Volunteers for Tom at the Capitol. Next to Tom is Dan
Enterline, chairman of Tom's campaign.

Judy McCabe was one of many volunteers, including George Jarvis, Bill Campbell, Phyllis Wyeth, Patti Hobbs, Annie Jones, Dirk Murchison and Dick and Gloria Prettyman, among others.

Bill Lickle, former chairman of the Delaware Trust Company, arranged for Tom to be finance chair in Delaware for Barry Goldwater's presidential bid in 1964.

Good friend Ron Olivere with Tom in Wilmington, Del.

John and Curt Riley, John Gehret and Tom after a round of
golf at Pine Valley Golf Club.

Tom and Mary Page campaigning with their children Page, Rob and Tommy.

Tom speaking at a campaign rally with daughter Page and Mary Page. Former Rep. Mike Castle is in the background.

Mary Page and Tom attending a masquerade ball.

At Mary Page's art show at Somerville Manning Gallery.
Tom is joined by daughter Page, Mary Page,
granddaughters Peyton and Katherine and son Tom.

Tom and Mary Page enjoying an evening with children Rob,
Page and Tom in Rehoboth Beach, Del.

Tom and Mary Page's grandchildren Peyton, Sam and
Katherine in Rehoboth Beach, Del.

Tom attending the Florida Derby.

Joe Biden with Tom's children Page and Tom along with
grandchildren Sam and Katherine.

Joe Biden attending Mary Page's art show opening at the
100th Anniversary of the Delaware Art Museum.

REFERENCES AND RESOURCES

1. "What They Are Saying About Tom Evans," *Tom Evans Action Line,* Winter 1975. Quoting Philadelphia Inquirer, 15 November 1975.

2. "He Made 'Em Mad at the White House," The Virginian-Pilot, 30 May 1973

3. Drew DeSilver, "The polarized Congress of today has its roots in the 1970s," Pew Research Center, https://www.pewresearch.org/fact-tank/2014/06/12/polarized-politics-in-congress-began-in-the-1970s-and-has-been-getting-worse-ever-since/. Accessed 20 October 2020

4. Pat Ordovensky, "House Panel Adopts Evans' Plan," The Morning News, 28 January 1977.

5. Gerard Colby, DuPont Dynasty: Behind the Nylon Curtain (New York: Open Road Media, 2014).

6. Trevor Goodloe, "LEON HOWARD SULLIVAN, JR. (1922-2001)," BlackPast, https://www.blackpast.org/african-american-history/sullivan-leon-howard-jr-1922-2001/. Accessed 20 October 2020.

7. Michael Rotman, "Cuyahoga River Fire," Cleveland Historical, https://clevelandhistorical.org/items/show/63. Accessed 20 October 2020.

8. "The Sixties," The Environmental History Timeline, http://environmentalhistory.org/20th-century/sixties-1960-1969/. Accessed 20 October 2020.

9. "The History of Earth Day," Earth Day Network, https://www.earthday.org/history/. Accessed 20 October 2020.

10. "The Origins of EPA," United States Environmental Protection Agency, https://www.epa.gov/history/origins-epa. Accessed 20 October 2020.

11. "40th Anniversary of the Clean Air Act," United States Environmental Protection Agency,

https://www.epa.gov/clean-air-act-overview/40th-anniversary-clean-air-act. Accessed 20 October 2020.

12. "'Love Canal' still oozing poison 35 years later," New York Post, https://nypost.com/2013/11/02/love-canal-still-oozing-poison-35-years-later/. Accessed 20 October 2020.

13. "H.R.4297 - A bill to amend the Marine Protection, Research, and Sanctuaries Act of 1972 to authorize appropriations to carry out the provisions of such Act for fiscal year 1978," Congress.gov, https://www.congress.gov/bill/95th-congress/house-bill/4297. Accessed 20 October 2020.

14. "Henry Eschwege, "Status of Effort to Phase out Ocean Dumping of Municipal Sewage Sludge," United States Government Accountability Office, http://archive.gao.gov/f0302/109826.pdf. Accessed 20 October 2020.

15. "Marine Protection, Research, and Sanctuaries Act of 1972," Wikipedia, https://en.wikipedia.org/wiki/Marine_Protection_,_Research,_and_Sanctuaries_Act_of_1972#Amendments. Accessed 20 October 2020.

16. "End of sludge dumping voted," The Morning News, 12 May 1977.

17. Sean Mclain Brown, "5 Reasons Why Chesty Puller is a Marine Corps Legend," Military.com, https://www.military.com/marine-corps/5-reasons-why-chesty-puller-marine-corps-legend.html. Accessed 20 October 2020.

18. "End of sludge dumping voted," The Morning News, 12 May 1977. http://www.newspapers.com/image/157879882. Accessed 20 October 2020.

19. Michael Fleming, "Tom Evans, the Art of Politics and the most important law nobody's ever heard of," Town Square Delaware, 22 April 2013.

20. "Alaska National Interest Lands Conservation Act," Wikipedia, https://en.wikipedia.org/wiki/Alaska_National_I

nterest_Lands_Conservation_Act. Accessed 20 October 2020.

21. Kyle Joly et al., "History, Purpose, and Status of Caribou Movements in Northwest Alaska," National Park Service, https://www.nps.gov/articles/aps-17-1-7.htm. Accessed 20 October 2020.

22. G. Frank Williss, "'Do Things Right the First Time' Administrative History: The National Park Service and the Alaska National Interest Lands Conservation Act of 1980," National Park Service, http://npshistory.com/centennial/0616/index.ht m. Accessed 20 October 2020.

23. "A victorious Evans says he won't fill a cabinet post," The Evening Journal, 5 November 1980.

24. Tom Evans, "The American and the Sea: How the government destroys barrier islands," The Washington Times, 10 September 1999.

25. "Coastal Barrier Resources Act," Wikipedia, https://en.wikipedia.org/wiki/Coastal_Barrier_R esources_Act. Accessed 20 October 2020.

26. John Sweeney, "Preserving the Shoreline," <u>The News Journal</u>, 28 June 2015.

27. Don Bonker with David Applefield , <u>A Higher Calling: Faith & Politics in the Public Square</u> (Nashville: Thomas Nelson, Elm Hill, 2019).

28. Kathy Canavan, "Hurricanes less lethal due to Tom Evans' legislation," <u>Delaware Business Times</u>, 17 October 2017.

29. Janet Hook and Natalie Andrews, "There Really Is a Secret Club in Washington Whose Members Run America," <u>The Wall Street Journal</u>, 20 June 2018, <u>https://www.wsj.com/articles/there-really-is-a-secret-club-in-washington-whose-members-run-america-1529506405.</u> Accessed 20 October 2020.

30. "Evans Acts as Policy Advisor," <u>Salisbury Times</u>, 14 April 1980.

31. "Reagan gets nod; Bush is VP pick," <u>The Morning News</u>, 17 July 1980.

32. Hugh Cutler and Margaret Clark, "A victorious Evans says he won't fill a Cabinet post," <u>Evening Journal, 5 November 1980.</u>

33. "H.R.3252 - Coastal Barrier Resources Act," Congress.gov, https://www.congress.gov/bill/97th-congress/house-bill/3252. Accessed 20 October 2020.

34. Congressional Record.

35. "Rebuilding the Shores, Increasing the Risk," The New York Times, 9 April 2013.

36. "Coastal Barrier Resources Act," Wikipedia, https://en.wikipedia.org/wiki/Coastal_Barrier_R esources_Act. Accessed 20 October 2020.

37. "CBRA Legislation and Testimony," United States Fish & Wildlife Service, https://www.fws.gov/cbra/Legislation.html. Accessed 20 October 2020.

38. Lois Romano, "Return from the Slough of Scandal," Washington Post, 5 June 1986.

39. Katharine Q. Seelye, "Edward Seaga, Who Led Jamaica on a Conservative Path, Dies at 89," The New York Times, 29 May 2019. https://www.nytimes.com/2019/05/29/obituarie

s/edward-seaga-dead.html. Accessed 20 October 2020.

40. Tom Evans, Alaska Conservation Foundation, December 2005, Speech.

41. Tom Evans, "Plan must combine clean energy, conservation," The News Journal, 1 December 2012.

42. Tom Evans, "The Sea's Power and Foolish Policies," The News Journal, 3 July 2015.

43. Tom Evans, "Scott Pruitt, 'Protecting his own environment,'" The New York Times, 25 April 2018.

44. "Briny Breezes - History of the 2007 Project," Florida Coalition for Preservation, http://www.preservationfla.org/brinybreezes_his tory.php. Accessed 20 October 2020.

45. Tom Evans, "Energy, Conservation and the Environment," Florida Atlantic University, 14 April 2005.

46. Tom Evans, "Count Them All Again," Washington Post, 18 November 2000.

47. Tom Evans, "Is Our Government Working for You?" Forum at Florida Atlantic University, 9 December 2006. Speech.

48. Tom Evans, Rotary Club of Wilmington, 29 September 2011. Speech.

49. "Trump is not the answer in a democracy" *The News Journal* Delaware Voice Monday, August 8, 2016 By Tom Evans

50. Diane Winston, "The History of the National Prayer Breakfast," Smithsonian Magazine, 2 February 2017. https://www.smithsonianmag.com/history/natio nal-prayer-breakfast-what-does-its-history-reveal-180962017/. Accessed 20 October 2020.

51. "Do YOU know Bermuda's racial history?" Bermuda Sun, 2 July 2013. http://bermudasun.bm/Content/NEWS/News/A rticle/Do-YOU-know-Bermuda-s-racial-history-/24/270/68036. Accessed 20 October 2020.

52. Prison Fellowship, https://www.prisonfellowship.org/. Accessed 20 October 2020.

53. Tom Evans, "Export-Import Bank Funds an Unwise Place to Trim," <u>Washington Star</u>, 5 July 1981.

54. Jack Ireland, "Captain Bodgit has locals dreaming of Roses," <u>The News Journal</u>, 18 March 1997.

55. "Ex-congressman still pulls strings on the Hill," <u>The News Journal</u>, 25 December 1997.

OTHER RESOURCES

U.S. Congress, House, Coastal Barrier Resources Act, Report together with Additional Views [To accompany S. 1018.], Report No. 97-419 (Washington: GPO, 1982), 3.

Pilkey, O. H., R. S. Young, J. Kelley, and A. D. Griffith. "Mining of coastal sand: a critical environmental and economic problem for morocco." White Paper (2007).

"Final Vote Result For Roll Call 419," United States House of Representatives, http://clerk.house.gov/evs/2018/roll419.xml. Accessed 17 August 2020.

"Coastal Barrier Resources Act," Govinfo, accessed August 17, 2020, https://www.govinfo.gov/content/pkg/STATUTE-96/pdf/STATUTE-96-Pg1653.pdf.

"Coastal Barrier Resources System: Changes to Flood Insurance Rate Maps," Federal Emergency Management Agency, accessed August 17, 2020, https://www.fema.gov/media-library-data/1549644052036-2d4a827900bd0d5a0ff05cd33ad580e5/FEMA_USFWS_CBRS_Fact_Sheet_REVISED_0131_2019_508.pdf.

"H.R.5787 - Strengthening Coastal Communities Act of 2018," Congress.gov, accessed August 17, 2020, https://www.congress.gov/bill/115th-congress/house-bill/5787.

"Marine Protection, Research, and Sanctuaries Act of 1972," Govinfo, accessed August 17, 2020, https://www.govinfo.gov/content/pkg/COMPS-1680/pdf/COMPS-1680.pdf.

Smother, Robert. "Sludge Composting Plan Raises Questions," The New York Times, accessed August 17, 2020, https://www.nytimes.com/1978/05/14/archives/westchester-weekly-sludge-composting-plan-raises-questions-sludge.html.

U.S. Congress, House, Coastal Barrier Resources Act, Report together with Additional Views [To accompany S. 1018.], Report No. 97-419 (Washington: GPO, 1982), 3.

ACKNOWLEDGMENTS

I'd like to thank John Sweeney who first brought this project to me and has been the behind-the-scenes support throughout the writing and publishing process. He tracked down long-buried documents to bring factual accuracy to the book and provided sage advice whenever it was needed.

To Daniel Villarreal, Grace Judson and Greg Sweeney for expert editing and feedback. They took the story and brought the words to life.

To Christina Cavillo and Chantal Towles for getting the documents into a usable form and being at the ready whenever I needed them.

To Sharon Baker and Manley Fuller for sharing personal stories of their relationship with Tom throughout the years. Their insights brought humanity to the story that balanced the many newspaper clippings and government reports.

To Page Evans Corey, who shared her writing, expertise and heartfelt stories of growing up in the Evans household.

To Mary Page Evans, who inspired me with her stories and artistic talents and encouraged both Tom and me to pursue the best version of this project.

And finally, to Tom, who invited me into his home and life and allowed me to tell his story. He spent hours sharing stories of days gone by and his vision for the future. He showed me what hard work can do and how, with perseverance, we can do even more. I witnessed, through his stories, how generosity of treasure, time and presence can make a lasting impact on people and the world. I am deeply grateful to him for sharing his life story with me.

Made in the USA
Columbia, SC
12 March 2021